THE
NINJA FOODI XL PRO

AIR FRYER OVEN

COOKBOOK FOR BEGINNERS

1000-DAY YUMMY, DELICIOUS AND TASTY RECIPES FOR FAMILY AND FRIENDS TO HAVE A BEST MEAL

MICHAEL KIRBY

CONTENTS

INTRODUCTION

What is and How the Ninja Foodi XL Pro Air Fryer Oven Works

Although standalone air frying appliances have become increasingly popular, the inconvenience of purchasing yet another countertop appliance that takes up extra room isn't always ideal. Fortunately, today's kitchen ranges come in a wide array of styles and configurations to allow for much more than simply baking cookies or casseroles. Many brands of gas and electric ranges now include air fryers that are built right into the oven.

You can cook up incredible feasts on a standard slide-in range, but what if you're looking for something more? Air fryer ranges offer a delicious-tasting alternative to preparing deep-fried foods. Unlike traditional deep fryers that use hot oil, air frying uses specialized convection fans to circulate hot air at high speeds when cooking your favorite foods. It cooks food faster while ensuring even browning on all sides. Best of all, it requires little to no oil compared to traditional deep fryers.

Air fryer ranges let you effortlessly change your oven's settings from conventional baking or heating to air frying. This is especially beneficial for frying up your favorite foods in less time. Both standalone and air fry range ovens work best with specialized cookware and bakeware like air fry trays, baking sheets or baskets that make the cooking process easy. Many air fryer ranges come with the cookware you'll need to begin making amazing meals right away!

Air fryer ovens circulate heat at super-fast rates to deliver faster cooking results. As stated before, they use convection fans to produce hot air and quickly distribute it evenly throughout the appliance. The main advantage of an air fryer oven over a convection oven is that it's better suited for creating that crispy fried taste much more successfully, especially since you use a specific type of basket or tray to help evenly circulate the heat around the food. For example, foods like chicken wings and French fries retain their natural texture and flavor in an air fryer range since the appliance is made to simulate a deep-fried cooking technique.

Benefits You'll Gain from Your Ninja Foodi XL Pro Air Fryer Oven

1. Drying food

As we all know, food such as melons and biscuits can become damp after a period at home, which affects the taste and seriously affects the storage time of the food, and the electric home oven can re-dry these wet food to the state we just bought. Delicious and healthy.

2. Snacking

Everyone loves food, especially children, who are particularly sensitive to snacking. If you have an electric oven at home, your child can bake bread and biscuits in it and deliciously enjoy the snacks.

3. You can also eat roast meat at home

With the right seasoning, you can grill at home. It's comfortable and clean to eat whatever you want.

4. Ferment dough and make chocolate treats

Put the dough that needs fermenting into an electric oven and set the temperature to the lowest possible setting to get it ready as quickly as possible. The same goes for chocolate, which can be melted and used in any way you like.

5. No oil, very healthy

For example, if you grill meat, you don't need to put oil in it, and during the grilling process, some of the meat's fat will be removed, so it's much healthier than frying or cooking in a pan.

6. Neat and clean

No more frying, no more frying, no more fumes, and no more clean kitchen.

7. Lazy people

When baking food, lay a layer of tinfoil on the baking tray and throw away the tinfoil when you're done, eliminating the need to brush the pan and wash the tray.

8. Keeping food warm

If you have an oven, you can keep the food warm in the oven. You can leave the stove on and use the preheating of the oven to keep the food warm.

Tips for Using Your Ninja Foodi XL Pro Air Fryer Oven

1. Remove all packing materials and stickers from the inside and outside of the appliance. Be sure that all accessories are included before throwing away any packaging. Remove wrapping from drip tray inside the oven.

2. Gently wipe the exterior of the oven with a clean, damp cloth and dry thoroughly.

3. Use a mild liquid soap and a damp cloth or sponge to wipe the interior walls. Note: Do not use abrasive cleaners, like steel wool pads, as they may damage the finish.

4. Hand wash the broil/baking pan, wire rack, air fryer basket and removable crumb/drip tray. All these accessories are top-rack dishwasher safe.

5. Place the appliance on a flat, heat-resistant surface.

6. Position the appliance at least 2-4" away from the wall or any objects on the countertop.

7. Do not use on heat-sensitive surfaces.

8. Always insert crumb/drip tray when operating appliance.

9. Metal, ovenproof glass or ceramic bakeware without glass lids can be used in the appliance. Be sure that the top of the container is at least 1 ½" away from the upper heating elements on the top interior.

Tips And Tricks on How to Clean Air Fryer Oven

Air fryer Ovens are much easier to clean than deep fryers that use lots of grease or oil. The cooking basket is closed to prevent spattering and any oil that is used goes into the oil pan to be discarded when dinner is over. With these units, air is the new oil! These cook up fish, chicken, and meat to crispy tender brown using a light batter, and are able to cook vegetables and fruit as well. Most of today's air fryers have some parts that go into the dishwasher. But if not, try these methods. Don't use knives, forks, or metal utensils to remove dried caked food from your air fryer. Most air fryers are coated inside with a non-stick product that's easy to ruin. Never use an abrasive cleaner.

Step 1. Wait until the air fryer cools to the touch and unplug it from the wall and the cooker, unless it is hard wired to the unit. Be sure all the old food is out of the interior pot. Never submerge the pot with plug electronics into water; it will be ruined forever.

Step 2. Cleaning the air fryer is uncomplicated. Wash the cooking basket, tray, and pan in dish-washing detergent in hot water. Most of the newer fryer component parts can go into the dishwasher, but not the housing with the electrical port. Wipe down the housing inside and out with dish-washing detergent, rinse, and towel dry.
Some air fryers have magnetic cord attachments to the bottom and some cords plug into the unit.

Step 3. If you have crusty hard food stuck to your air fryer, make a paste of baking soda and water and scrub gently with a sponge or cloth, rinse, and towel dry. You can use this paste gently on the heating element with an old soft toothbrush at the bottom of your air fryer.

Step 4. Let all parts and the air fryer air dry for a few hours too before putting it away.
Tip: Clean the air fryer after each time it's used; don't wait until it's a hard stuck-on mess before cleaning.

Note: The ceramic, stoneware, and lid will not endure abrupt changes in temperature. Therefore, do not fill a hot pot with cold water; it can crack. Ceramic and stoneware are porous materials and when submerged in water over the top, water can enter the material. I did that to one of my baking dishes and it looks horrible now. The bowl can be filled with water and sit but not submerged in water.

BREAKFAST

Savory Breakfast Bread Pudding

Servings: 4

Cooking Time: 30 Minutes

Ingredients:

- Oil spray (hand-pumped)
- 4 slices whole-wheat bread, cubed
- 1 cup frozen potato hash browns, thawed
- 5 large eggs
- 1 cup whole milk
- ½ cup diced ham
- ½ cup shredded cheddar cheese
- 1 teaspoon fresh parsley, chopped
- ⅛ teaspoon sea salt
- ⅛ teaspoon freshly ground black pepper

Directions:

1. Place the baking tray on position 1 and preheat the toaster oven on BAKE to 350°F for 5 minutes.
2. Lightly oil an 8-inch-square baking dish with spray.
3. Spread the bread cubes and potatoes in the baking dish evenly.
4. In a medium bowl, combine the eggs, milk, ham, cheese, parsley, salt, and pepper.
5. Pour the egg mixture over the bread and potatoes in the dish.
6. Bake for 30 minutes. The bread pudding should be lightly golden, the eggs set, and a knife inserted in the center should come out clean.
7. Cool the pudding for 5 minutes and serve.

Freezer-ready Breakast Burritos

Servings: 8   Cooking Time: 28 Minutes

Ingredients:

- 8 large eggs
- 2 tablespoons whole milk
- Kosher salt and freshly ground black pepper
- 1 tablespoon unsalted butter
- 1 pound bulk breakfast sausage
- 1 medium russet potato, peeled and finely chopped
- 2 green onions, white and green portions, chopped
- 8 flour tortillas, about 8 inches in diameter
- 1 cup shredded sharp cheddar cheese
- Salsa
- Optional toppings: guacamole, chopped avocado, chopped tomato

Directions:

1. Whisk the eggs and milk in a large bowl and season with salt and pepper. Melt the butter in a large skillet over medium heat. Add the eggs and cook, stirring occasionally, until the eggs are softly set. Spoon the cooked eggs into a medium bowl; set aside.

2. Cook the sausage in the same skillet over medium heat until lightly browned, stirring to crumble. Add the potato and cook, stirring frequently, until the sausage is fully cooked and the potato is tender. Stir in the green onions and cook for 2 minutes. Drain.

3. Wrap the tortillas in a clean towel and microwave on High (100 percent power) for 90 seconds or until warm.

4. Spoon the sausage-vegetable mixture, eggs, and cheese evenly into each tortilla. Fold in the sides of the tortilla, then roll gently to form a burrito. Wrap each burrito in aluminum foil, then seal in a freezer bag or container. Label and freeze for up to 1 month.

5. The night before serving, place the number of wrapped burritos you wish to serve in the refrigerator to partially thaw.

6. Preheat the toaster oven to 375°F. Place the foil-wrapped burrito on the rack in the toaster oven. Bake for 20 to 25 minutes or until heated through. Carefully unwrap the burrito and place on a plate. Top with salsa and any of the suggested toppings.

Fry Bread

Servings: 4

Cooking Time: 5 Minutes

Ingredients:

- 1 cup flour
- 2 teaspoons baking powder
- ¼ teaspoon salt
- ¼ cup lukewarm milk
- 1 teaspoon oil
- 2–3 tablespoons water
- oil for misting or cooking spray

Directions:

1. Stir together flour, baking powder, and salt. Gently mix in the milk and oil. Stir in 1 tablespoon water. If needed, add more water 1 tablespoon at a time until stiff dough forms. Dough shouldn't be sticky, so use only as much as you need.

2. Divide dough into 4 portions and shape into balls. Cover with a towel and let rest for 10 minutes.

3. Preheat the toaster oven to 390°F.

4. Shape dough as desired:

5. a. Pat into 3-inch circles. This will make a thicker bread to eat plain or with a sprinkle of cinnamon or honey butter. You can cook all 4 at once.

6. b. Pat thinner into rectangles about 3 x 6 inches. This will create a thinner bread to serve as a base for dishes such as Indian tacos. The circular shape is more traditional, but rectangles allow you to cook 2 at a time in your air fryer oven.

7. Spray both sides of dough pieces with oil or cooking spray.

8. Place the 4 circles or 2 of the dough rectangles in the air fryer oven and air-fry at 390°F for 3 minutes. Spray tops, turn, spray other side, and air fry for 2 more minutes. If necessary, repeat to cook remaining bread.

9. Serve piping hot as is or allow to cool slightly and add toppings to create your own Native American tacos.

Cinnamon Sugar Donut Holes

Servings: 12

Cooking Time: 6 Minutes

Ingredients:

- 1 cup all-purpose flour
- 6 tablespoons cane sugar, divided
- 1 teaspoon baking powder
- 3 teaspoons ground cinnamon, divided
- ¼ teaspoon salt
- 1 large egg
- 1 teaspoon vanilla extract
- 2 tablespoons melted butter

Directions:

1. Preheat the toaster oven to 370°F.

2. In a small bowl, combine the flour, 2 tablespoons of the sugar, the baking powder, 1 teaspoon of the cinnamon, and the salt. Mix well.

3. In a larger bowl, whisk together the egg, vanilla extract, and butter.

4. Slowly add the dry ingredients into the wet until all the ingredients are uniformly combined. Set the bowl inside the refrigerator for at least 30 minutes.

5. Before you're ready to cook, in a small bowl, mix together the remaining 4 tablespoons of sugar and 2 teaspoons of cinnamon.

6. Liberally spray the air fryer oven with olive oil mist so the donut holes don't stick to the bottom.

7. Remove the dough from the refrigerator and divide it into 12 equal donut holes. You can use a 1-ounce serving scoop if you have one.

8. Roll each donut hole in the sugar and cinnamon mixture; then place in the air fryer oven. Repeat until all the donut holes are covered in the sugar and cinnamon mixture.

9. When the oven is full, air-fry for 6 minutes. Remove the donut holes from the oven using oven-safe tongs and let cool 5 minutes. Repeat until all 12 are cooked.

Creamy Bacon + Almond Crostini

Servings: 20

Cooking Time: 10 Minutes

Ingredients:

- ➢ 1 baguette loaf, cut into ½-inch-thick slices
- ➢ 2 tablespoons olive oil
- ➢ 4 ounces cream cheese, cut into cubes, softened
- ➢ ½ cup mayonnaise
- ➢ 1 cup shredded fontina cheese or Monterey Jack cheese
- ➢ 4 slices bacon, cooked until crisp and crumbled
- ➢ 1 green onion, white and green portions, finely chopped
- ➢ ¼ teaspoon Sriracha or hot sauce
- ➢ Dash kosher salt
- ➢ ¼ cup sliced almonds, toasted
- ➢ Minced fresh flat-leaf (Italian) parsley

Directions:

1. Toast the slices of the baguette in the toaster oven.

2. Arrange the toasted baguette slices on a 12-inch pizza pan or a 12 x 12-inch baking pan. Lightly brush the slices with the olive oil.

3. Preheat the toaster oven to 375°F.

4. Beat the cream cheese and mayonnaise in a medium bowl with an electric mixer at medium speed until creamy and smooth. Stir in the fontina, bacon, green onion, Sriracha, and salt and blend until combined.

5. Distribute the cheese mixture evenly over the toasted bread. Top with the sliced almonds. Bake for 6 to 8 minutes or until the cheese is hot and beginning to melt. Allow to cool for 1 to 2 minutes, then garnish with minced parsley. Serve warm.

Yogurt Bread

Servings: 2

Cooking Time: 40 Minutes

Ingredients:

- ➤ 3 cups unbleached flour
- ➤ 4 teaspoons baking powder
- ➤ 5 2 teaspoons sugar
- ➤ Salt to taste
- ➤ 1 cup plain nonfat yogurt
- ➤ ¼ cup vegetable oil
- ➤ 1 egg, beaten, to brush the top

Directions:

1. Preheat the toaster oven to 375° F.

2. Combine the flour, baking powder, sugar, and salt in a large bowl. Make a hole in the center and spoon in the yogurt and oil.

3. Stir the flour into the center. When the dough is well mixed, turn it out onto a lightly floured surface and knead for 8 minutes, until the dough is smooth and elastic. Place the dough in an oiled or nonstick regular-size 8½ × 4½ × 2¼-inch loaf pan. Brush the top with the beaten egg.

4. BAKE for 40 minutes, or until a toothpick inserted in the center comes out clean and the loaf is browned. Invert on a wire rack to cool.

Italian Strata

Servings: 6

Cooking Time: 55 Minutes

Ingredients:

- 1 cup boiling water
- 3 tablespoons chopped sun-dried tomatoes (dry-packed)
- 5 cups cubed French bread or country bread (cut into 1-inch cubes)
- Nonstick cooking spray
- 1 ½ ounces sliced turkey pepperoni, cut into fourths (about ¾ cup)
- 2 tablespoons chopped pepperoncini peppers
- 1 cup coarsely chopped fresh spinach
- 1 cup shredded Italian blend cheese or mozzarella cheese
- 4 large eggs
- 1 ½ cups whole milk
- 1 teaspoon Italian seasoning
- ¼ teaspoon kosher salt
- 2 tablespoons shredded Parmesan cheese

Directions:

1. Pour the boiling water the over sun-dried tomatoes in a small, deep bowl; set aside.

2. Preheat the toaster oven to 350 °F. Place the bread cubes on a 12 x 12-inch baking pan. Bake for 10 minutes, stirring once.

3. Spray an 8 x 8-inch square baking pan with nonstick cooking spray. Drain the sun-dried tomatoes and pat dry with paper towels. Arrange half the bread cubes evenly in the prepared pan. Top with half the pepperoni, half the pepperoncini, all the spinach, and all of the reconstituted tomatoes. Sprinkle with ½ cup of the Italian cheese. Repeat layers with the remaining bread, pepperoni, pepperoncini, and ½ cup cheese.

4. Whisk the eggs, milk, Italian seasoning, and salt in a large bowl. Pour the egg mixture over the bread layers. Press down lightly with the back of a large spoon. Sprinkle with the Parmesan cheese. Cover and chill for at least 2 hours or overnight.

5. Preheat the toaster oven to 350°F. Bake the strata, uncovered, for 35 to 45 minutes, or until a knife inserted into the center comes out clean. Let stand for 10 minutes before serving.

Quick Fruit And Raisin Bread

Servings: 6

Cooking Time: 35 Minutes

Ingredients:

- ➢ 2 cups unbleached flour
- ➢ 3 tablespoons margarine
- ➢ 4 ¾ cup low-fat buttermilk
- ➢ 5 teaspoons baking powder
- ➢ 1 egg, beaten
- ➢ 2 tablespoons honey
- ➢ ¼ cup chopped raisins
- ➢ ½ cup chopped dried fruit
- ➢ 3 tablespoons chopped almonds
- ➢ 4 ½ teaspoon grated nutmeg
- ➢ Salt to taste

Directions:

1. Preheat the toaster oven to 400° F.

2. Combine all the ingredients in a large bowl, stirring well. Pour the batter into an oiled or nonstick regular-size 8½ × 4½ × ⅔-inch loaf pan or 2 small-size 3½ × 7½ × 2¼-inch loaf pans.

3. BAKE for 35 minutes, or until a toothpick inserted in the center comes out clean.

French Toast Sticks

Servings: 4

Cooking Time: 8 Minutes

Ingredients:

- 2 eggs
- ¼ cup half-and-half
- ½ teaspoon vanilla extract
- 6 slices wheat bread, cut into 1-inch strips
- 1 teaspoon ground cinnamon
- 2 tablespoons granulated sugar
- Maple syrup or pureed strawberries for serving

Directions:

1. In an 8-x-12-inch casserole dish, whisk together the eggs, half-and-half, and vanilla. Lay the strips of bread into the baking dish and flip around. Allow the bread to soak up the egg mixture for 10 minutes.
2. Meanwhile, in a small bowl, stir together the cinnamon and sugar.
3. Place the soaked bread strips into the air fryer oven, not touching one another. Spray with cooking spray and sprinkle the cinnamon and sugar mixture onto the bread sticks.
4. Air fry the French toast sticks at 370°F for 8 minutes. Cook in batches, as needed.
5. Serve with maple syrup or pureed strawberries.

Brunch Burritos

Servings: 4

Cooking Time: 14 Minutes

Ingredients:

- ➢ Egg mixture:
- ➢ 4 medium eggs, lightly beaten
- ➢ 3 tablespoons finely chopped bell pepper
- ➢ 2 tablespoons finely chopped onion
- ➢ 4 strips lean turkey bacon, uncooked and cut into small ¼ × ¼-inch pieces
- ➢ 1 tablespoon chopped fresh cilantro
- ➢ ½ teaspoon ground cumin
- ➢ ½ teaspoon chili powder
- ➢ Salt and red pepper flakes to taste
- ➢ 4 6-inch flour tortillas
- ➢ 4 tablespoons salsa
- ➢ 4 tablespoons shredded part-skim, low-moisture mozzarella

Directions:

1. Combine the egg mixture ingredients in an oiled or nonstick 8½ × 8½ × 2-inch square baking (cake) pan.

2. TOAST twice, or until the mixture is firm and cooked.

3. Spoon the egg mixture in equal portions onto the center of each tortilla. Add 1 tablespoon salsa and 1 tablespoon mozzarella cheese to each. Roll each tortilla around the filling and lay, seam side down, in an oiled or nonstick 8½ × 8½ × 2-inch square baking (cake) pan.

4. BROIL for 8 minutes, or until lightly browned.

French Toast Casserole

Servings: 6

Cooking Time: 60 Minutes

Ingredients:

- 1 tablespoon unsalted butter, softened, plus 6 tablespoons unsalted butter, melted, divided
- ¾ cup packed (5¼ ounces) brown sugar
- 1 tablespoon ground cinnamon
- ½ teaspoon ground nutmeg
- ⅛ teaspoon table salt
- 18 slices potato sandwich bread, divided
- 2½ cups whole milk
- 6 large eggs
- ¼ cup sliced almonds, toasted
- Confectioners' sugar

Directions:

1. Adjust toaster oven rack to middle position and preheat the toaster oven to 350 degrees. Grease 13 by 9-inch baking dish with softened butter. Mix brown sugar, cinnamon, nutmeg, and salt together in bowl.

2. Sprinkle 3 tablespoons brown sugar mixture evenly over bottom of prepared dish. Place 6 bread slices (use bread heels here) in even layer in bottom of dish. Brush bread with 1½ tablespoons melted butter and sprinkle with 3 tablespoons sugar mixture.

3. Place 6 bread slices in single layer over first layer, brush with 1½ tablespoons melted butter, then sprinkle with 3 tablespoons sugar mixture. Place remaining 6 bread slices over previous layer and brush with 1½ tablespoons melted butter.

4. In separate bowl, whisk milk and eggs until well combined, then pour evenly over bread. Gently press down on layers with spatula to saturate bread. (Casserole can be covered and refrigerated for up to 12 hours.)

5. Sprinkle with almonds and remaining sugar mixture. Bake until casserole is slightly puffed and golden brown and bubbling around edges, 30 to 35 minutes, rotating dish halfway through baking. Transfer dish to wire rack, brush with remaining 1½ tablespoons melted butter, and let cool for 15 minutes. Sprinkle with confectioners' sugar and serve.

Strawberry Pie

Servings: 6

Cooking Time: 25 Minutes

Ingredients:

- 2 16-ounce packages frozen sliced strawberries or 1 quart fresh strawberries, washed, stemmed, and sliced
- ¼ cup sugar
- 2 tablespoons lemon juice
- 2 tablespoons cornstarch
- 1 single Oatmeal Piecrust, baked (recipe follows)
- Strawberry Pie Glaze (recipe follows)

Directions:

1. Preheat the toaster oven to 350° F.

2. Combine the strawberries, sugar, lemon juice, and cornstarch in a medium bowl, mixing well. Fill the piecrust shell with the strawberries, spreading evenly.

3. BAKE for 25 minutes, or until the strawberries are tender. Glaze with Strawberry Pie Glaze.

LUNCH AND DINNER

Honey Bourbon–glazed Pork Chops With Sweet Potatoes + Apples

Servings: 2   Cooking Time: 42 Minutes

Ingredients:

- Nonstick cooking spray
- 2 medium sweet potatoes, peeled and quartered
- 2 tablespoons bourbon
- 2 tablespoons honey
- 1 tablespoon canola or vegetable oil
- ½ teaspoon onion powder
- ½ teaspoon dry mustard
- ¼ teaspoon dried thyme leaves
- Kosher salt and freshly ground black pepper
- 2 bone-in pork chops, cut about ¾ inch thick
- 1 Granny Smith apple, not peeled, cored and cut into ½-inch wedges

Directions:

1. Preheat the toaster oven to 375°F. Spray a 12 x 12-inch baking pan with nonstick cooking spray.

2. Place the sweet potatoes on one side of the prepared pan. Spray with nonstick cooking spray. Bake, uncovered, for 20 minutes.

3. Meanwhile, stir the bourbon, honey, oil, onion powder, mustard, and thyme in a small bowl. Season with salt and pepper and set aside.

4. Turn the potatoes over. Place the pork chops on the other end of the pan in a single layer. Arrange the apple wedges around the potatoes and pork chops, stacking the apples as needed. Brush the bourbon mixture generously over all. Bake for 15 to 18 minutes or until the pork is done as desired and a meat thermometer registers a minimum of 145°F.

5. For additional browning, set the toaster oven to Broil and broil for 2 to 4 minutes, or until the edges are brown as desired.

6. Transfer to a serving platter. Spoon any drippings over the meat and vegetables. Let stand for 5 minutes before serving.

Rosemary Lentils

Servings: 2

Cooking Time: 35 Minutes

Ingredients:

- ¼ cup lentils
- 1 tablespoon mashed Roasted Garlic
- 1 rosemary sprig
- 1 bay leaf
- Salt and freshly ground black pepper
- 2 tablespoons low-fat buttermilk
- 2 tablespoons tomato sauce

Directions:

1. Preheat the toaster oven to 400° F.

2. Combine the lentils, 1¼ cups water, garlic, rosemary sprig, and bay leaf in a 1-quart 8½ × 8½ × 4-inch ovenproof baking dish, stirring to blend well. Add the salt and pepper to taste. Cover with aluminum foil.

3. BAKE, covered, for 35 minutes, or until the lentils are tender. Remove the rosemary sprig and bay leaf and stir in the buttermilk and tomato sauce. Serve immediately.

Oven-baked Rice

Servings: 2

Cooking Time: 40 Minutes

Ingredients:

- ¼ cup regular rice (not parboiled or precooked)
- Seasonings:
- 1 tablespoon olive oil
- 1 teaspoon dried parsley or
- 1 tablespoon chopped fresh parsley
- 1 teaspoon garlic powder or roasted garlic
- Salt and freshly ground black pepper to taste

Directions:

1. Preheat the toaster oven to 400° F.

2. Combine ¼ cups water and the rice in a 1-quart 8½ × 8½ × 4-inch ovenproof baking dish. Stir well to blend. Cover with aluminum foil.

3. BAKE, covered, for 30 minutes, or until the rice is almost cooked. Add the seasonings, fluff with a fork to combine the seasonings well, then let the rice sit, covered, for 10 minutes. Fluff once more before serving.

Roasted Harissa Chicken + Vegetables

Servings: 4

Cooking Time: 30 Minutes

Ingredients:

- Nonstick cooking spray
- 1 medium zucchini, halved lengthwise and sliced crosswise ½ inch thick
- ½ large red onion, sliced ¼ inch thick
- 2 tablespoons olive oil
- Kosher salt and freshly ground black pepper
- 1 pound boneless, skinless chicken breasts, cut into 1-inch cubes
- ½ teaspoon ground cumin
- 1 clove garlic, minced
- 2 tablespoons harissa sauce or paste
- 1 tablespoon honey
- 2 tablespoons minced fresh cilantro
- 2 cups hot cooked rice
- Optional toppings: plain Greek yogurt or sour cream, sesame seeds (toasted or chopped), or dry-roasted peanuts

Directions:

1. Preheat the toaster oven to 400°F. Spray a 12 x 12-inch baking pan with nonstick cooking spray.

2. Place the zucchini and red onion in a medium bowl. Drizzle with 1 tablespoon olive oil and season with salt and pepper. Stir to coat the vegetables evenly. Arrange the vegetables in a single layer in the prepared baking pan. Roast, uncovered, for 10 minutes.

3. Place the chicken cubes in that same bowl. Drizzle with the remaining 1 tablespoon olive oil. Season with the cumin, garlic, salt, and pepper. Stir to coat the chicken evenly.

4. Stir the vegetables and move to one side of the pan. Arrange the chicken in a single layer on the other side of the pan. Roast for 10 minutes.

5. Blend the harissa and honey in a small bowl. Drizzle the sauce over the chicken and vegetables. Using a pastry brush, coat the chicken and vegetables evenly. Roast, uncovered, for an additional 8 to 10 minutes, or until the vegetables are tender and the chicken registers 165°F on a meat thermometer.

6. Spoon the chicken, vegetables, and any collected liquid onto a serving platter. Sprinkle with the cilantro. Serve the chicken and vegetables with the rice and, if desired, a dollop of plain Greek yogurt and a sprinkling of sesame seeds.

Sage, Chicken + Mushroom Pasta Casserole

Servings: 6

Cooking Time: 35 Minutes

Ingredients:

- Nonstick cooking spray
- 8 ounces bow-tie pasta, uncooked
- 4 tablespoons unsalted butter
- 8 ounces button or white mushrooms, sliced
- 3 tablespoons all-purpose flour
- Kosher salt and freshly ground black pepper
- 2 cups whole milk
- ½ cup dry white wine
- 2 tablespoons minced fresh sage
- 1 ½ cups chopped cooked chicken
- 1 cup shredded fontina, Monterey Jack, or Swiss cheese
- ½ cup shredded Parmesan cheese

Directions:

1. Preheat the toaster oven to 350°F. Spray a 2-quart baking pan with nonstick cooking spray.

2. Cook the pasta according to the package directions; drain and set aside.

3. Melt the butter in a large skillet over medium-high heat. Add the mushrooms and cook, stirring frequently, until the liquid has evaporated, 7 to 10 minutes. Blend in the flour and cook, stirring constantly, for 1 minute. Season with salt and pepper. Gradually stir in the milk and wine. Cook, stirring constantly, until the mixture bubbles and begins to thicken. Remove from the heat. Stir in the sage, cooked pasta, chicken, and fontina. Season with salt and pepper.

4. Spoon into the prepared pan. Cover and bake for 25 to 30 minutes. Uncover, sprinkle with the Parmesan, and bake for an additional 5 minutes or until the cheese is melted.

5. Remove from the oven and let stand for 5 to 10 minutes before serving.

Family Favorite Pizza

Servings: 6

Cooking Time: 22 Minutes

Ingredients:

- ➢ CRUST
- ➢ ½ cup warm water (about 110 ºF)
- ➢ 1 teaspoon active dry yeast
- ➢ 1 ½ cups all-purpose flour, plus more for kneading
- ➢ 1 teaspoon kosher salt
- ➢ ½ teaspoon olive oil
- ➢ TOPPINGS
- ➢ Pizza sauce
- ➢ 2 cups shredded Italian blend cheese or mozzarella cheese
- ➢ ¼ cup grated Parmesan cheese
- ➢ Optional toppings: pepperoni slices, cooked crumbled or sliced sausage, vegetables, or other favorite pizza toppings

Directions:

1. Make the Crust: Pour the water into a medium bowl and sprinkle with the yeast. Let stand for 5 minutes until the yeast is foamy. Add the flour, salt, and olive oil. Mix until a dough forms. Turn the dough out on a floured surface and knead until a ball forms that springs back when you poke a finger into it, about 5 minutes. If the dough is too sticky, add a tablespoon of flour and knead into the dough. Cover the dough and allow to rest for 10 minutes.

2. Preheat the toaster oven to 450°F. Place a 12-inch pizza pan in the toaster oven while it is preheating.

3. Stretch and roll the dough into an 11 ½-inch round. If the dough starts to shrink back, let it rest for 5 to 10 more minutes and then continue to roll. Carefully remove the hot pan from the toaster oven and place the pizza crust on the hot pan. Top with the desired amount of sauce. Layer cheese and any of your favorite pizza toppings over the pizza.

4. Bake for 18 to 22 minutes, or until the crust is golden brown and the cheese is melted. Let stand for 5 minutes before cutting.

Fresh Herb Veggie Pizza

Servings: 4

Cooking Time: 25 Minutes

Ingredients:

- 1 9-inch ready-made pizza crust
- 1 tablespoon olive oil
- 1 4-ounce can tomato paste
- 2 tablespoons shredded part-skim mozzarella
- 2 tablespoons grated Parmesan cheese
- 2 tablespoons crumbled feta cheese
- ½ bell pepper, chopped
- 1 tablespoon chopped fresh parsley
- 1 tablespoon chopped fresh oregano
- 1 tablespoon chopped fresh basil
- ½ teaspoon red pepper flakes
- Salt and freshly ground black pepper to taste
- Pizza mixture:
- 2 garlic cloves, minced
- 1 plum tomato, chopped

Directions:

1. Preheat the toaster oven to 400° F.
2. Brush the pizza crust with olive oil and spread the tomato paste evenly to cover.
3. Combine the ingredients for the pizza mixture and spread evenly on top of the tomato paste layer. Sprinkle the cheeses over all and season to taste. Place the pizza on the toaster oven rack.
4. BAKE for 25 minutes, or until the vegetables are cooked and the cheese is melted.

Sheet Pan Beef Fajitas

Servings: 3

Cooking Time: 10 Minutes

Ingredients:

- ➢ Nonstick cooking spray
- ➢ 3 tablespoons olive oil
- ➢ 1 ½ teaspoons chili powder
- ➢ 2 teaspoons ground cumin
- ➢ 1 teaspoon kosher salt
- ➢ 1 onion, halved and sliced into ¼-inch strips
- ➢ 1 large red or green bell pepper, cut into thin strips
- ➢ ¾-pound flank steak, cut across the grain into thin strips
- ➢ 3 tablespoons fresh lime juice
- ➢ 3 cloves garlic, minced
- ➢ 6 flour or corn tortillas, warmed

Directions:

1. Position the rack to broil. Preheat the toaster oven on the Broil setting. Spray a 12 x 12-inch baking pan with nonstick cooking spray.

2. Combine the olive oil, chili powder, cumin, and salt in a small bowl. Add the onion and bell pepper and toss to coat them evenly with the mixture. Use a slotted spoon to remove the vegetables from the seasoned oil mixture. Reserve the seasoned oil mixture. Place the vegetables in a single layer on the prepared pan. Broil for about 5 minutes or until the vegetables are beginning to brown.

3. Meanwhile, toss the steak strips in the reserved seasoned oil mixture. Push the vegetables to one side of the pan and add the steak in a single layer on the other side of the pan. Broil for 5 minutes.

4. When the meat is done, remove the meat from the pan and toss with the lime juice and garlic. Serve the meat and vegetables in warm tortillas.

Moroccan Couscous

Servings: 4

Cooking Time: 22 Minutes

Ingredients:

- ➤ 1 cup couscous
- ➤ 2 tablespoons finely chopped scallion
- ➤ 2 tablespoons finely chopped bell pepper
- ➤ 1 plum tomato, finely chopped
- ➤ 2 tablespoons chopped pitted black olives
- ➤ 1 tablespoon olive oil
- ➤ ¼ teaspoon ground cumin
- ➤ ¼ teaspoon ground cinnamon
- ➤ ¼ teaspoon turmeric Pinch of cayenne
- ➤ Salt and freshly ground black pepper to taste

Directions:

1. Preheat the toaster oven to 400° F.

2. Combine all the ingredients with ¼ cups water in a 1-quart 8½ × 8½ × 4-inch ovenproof baking dish. Adjust the seasonings to taste. Cover with aluminum foil.

3. BAKE, covered, for 12 minutes. Remove from the heat and fluff with a fork. Cover again and let stand for 10 minutes. Fluff once more before serving.

Yeast Dough For Two Pizzas

Servings: 8

Cooking Time: 20 Minutes

Ingredients:

- ¼ cup tepid water
- 1 cup tepid skim milk
- ½ teaspoon sugar
- 1 1¼-ounce envelope dry yeast
- 2 cups unbleached flour
- 1 tablespoon olive oil

Directions:

1. Preheat the toaster oven to 400° F.

2. Combine the water, milk, and sugar in a bowl. Add the yeast and set aside for 3 to 5 minutes, or until the yeast is dissolved.

3. Stir in the flour gradually, adding just enough to form a ball of the dough.

4. KNEAD on a floured surface until the dough is satiny, and then put the dough in a bowl in a warm place with a damp towel over the top. In 1 hour or when the dough has doubled in bulk, punch it down and divide it in half. Flatten the dough and spread it out to the desired thickness on an oiled or nonstick 9¾-inch-diameter pie pan. Spread with Homemade Pizza Sauce (recipe follows) and add any desired toppings.

5. BAKE for 20 minutes, or until the topping ingredients are cooked and the cheese is melted.

Homemade Beef Enchiladas

Servings: 4

Cooking Time: 20 Minutes

Ingredients:

- 1 tablespoon canola or vegetable oil
- 1 tablespoon plus 1 teaspoon all-purpose flour
- 2 tablespoons chili powder
- ½ teaspoon ground cumin
- ½ teaspoon garlic powder
- ¼ teaspoon kosher salt
- 1 ¼ cups chicken or vegetable broth
- ¾ pound lean ground beef
- Nonstick cooking spray
- 8 flour or corn tortillas
- ¼ cup finely chopped onion
- 1 ½ cups shredded Mexican-blend or cheddar cheese

Directions:

1. Heat the oil in a small saucepan over medium-high heat. Add the flour and whisk for about a minute. Stir in the chili powder, cumin, garlic powder, and salt. Gradually stir in the broth, whisking until smooth. Reduce the heat to a simmer and cook the sauce for 10 to 12 minutes.

2. Cook the ground beef in a medium skillet over medium-high heat until browned and cooked through, stirring to crumble into a fine texture. Remove from the heat and drain.

3. Preheat the toaster oven to 350°F. Spray an 11 x 7 x 2 ½-inch baking dish with nonstick cooking spray. Place about ½ cup sauce over the bottom of the dish. Lay a tortilla on a large plate and spread about 2 tablespoons of sauce over the surface of the tortilla. Spoon 2 tablespoons of the ground beef down the center of the tortilla. Sprinkle with some onion and cheese (amount is up to you). Roll up and place in the baking dish. Repeat with the remaining tortillas. Pour the remaining sauce over the top. Sprinkle with remaining cheese. Bake, uncovered, for 20 minutes or until the tortillas are heated through and slightly crisp on the outside.

Creamy Roasted Pepper Basil Soup

Servings: 4

Cooking Time: 35 Minutes

Ingredients:

- 1 5-ounce jar roasted peppers, drained ½ cup fresh basil leaves
- 1 cup fat-free half-and-half
- 1 cup skim milk
- 2 tablespoons reduced-fat cream cheese
- 1 teaspoon garlic powder
- 1 teaspoon paprika
- Salt and freshly ground black pepper to taste
- 2 tablespoons chopped fresh basil leaves (garnish for cold soup)
- 2 tablespoons grated Parmesan cheese (topping for hot soup)

Directions:

1. Preheat the toaster oven to 400° F.
2. Process all the ingredients in a blender or food processor until smooth. Transfer the mixture to a 1-quart 8½ × 8½ × 4-inch ovenproof baking dish.
3. BAKE, covered, for 35 minutes. Ladle into individual soup bowls and serve.

Healthy Southwest Stuffed Peppers

Servings: 6

Cooking Time: 30 Minutes

Ingredients:

- 1 tablespoon oil
- 1 small onion, chopped
- 1 garlic clove, minced
- 1/2 pound ground turkey
- 1/2 cup drained black beans
- 1/2 cup whole kernel corn
- 1 jar (16 oz.) medium salsa, divided
- 1/2 cup cooked white rice
- 1/2 teaspoon chili powder
- 1/2 teaspoon salt
- 1/4 teaspoon ground cumin
- 1/4 teaspoon black pepper
- 3 medium peppers, halved lengthwise leaving stem on, seeded
- 1/3 cup shredded Monterey Jack cheese, divided
- Sour cream
- Chopped fresh cilantro

Directions:

1. Preheat the toaster oven to 350°F. Spray baking pan with nonstick cooking spray.
2. In a large skillet over medium-high, heat oil. Add onion and garlic, cook for 2 to 3 minutes.
3. Add turkey to skillet, cook, stirring frequently, for 6 to 8 minutes or until turkey is cooked through.
4. Stir black beans, corn, 1/2 cup salsa, rice, chili powder, salt, cumin and pepper into turkey mixture.
5. Fill each pepper half with turkey mixture, dividing mixture evenly among peppers.
6. Top each pepper half with remaining salsa.
7. Bake 20 minutes. Sprinkle with cheese and bake an additional 10 minutes or until heated through.
8. Top with sour cream and cilantro.

FISH AND SEAFOOD

Maple-crusted Salmon

Servings: 2

Cooking Time: 8 Minutes

Ingredients:

- 12 ounces salmon filets
- ⅓ cup maple syrup
- 1 teaspoon Worcestershire sauce
- 2 teaspoons Dijon mustard or brown mustard
- ½ cup finely chopped walnuts
- ½ teaspoon sea salt
- ½ lemon
- 1 tablespoon chopped parsley, for garnish

Directions:

1. Place the salmon in a shallow baking dish. Top with maple syrup, Worcestershire sauce, and mustard. Refrigerate for 30 minutes.

2. Preheat the toaster oven to 350°F.

3. Remove the salmon from the marinade and discard the marinade.

4. Place the chopped nuts on top of the salmon filets, and sprinkle salt on top of the nuts. Place the salmon, skin side down, in the air fryer oven. Air-fry for 6 to 8 minutes or until the fish flakes in the center.

5. Remove the salmon and plate on a serving platter. Squeeze fresh lemon over the top of the salmon and top with chopped parsley. Serve immediately.

Crab-stuffed Peppers

Servings: 4

Cooking Time: 45 Minutes

Ingredients:

➢ Filling:

➢ 1½ cups fresh crabmeat, chopped, or 2 6-ounce cans lump crabmeat, drained

➢ 4 plum tomatoes, chopped

➢ 2 4-ounce cans sliced mushrooms, drained well

➢ 4 tablespoons pitted and sliced black olives

➢ 2 tablespoons olive oil

➢ 2 garlic cloves, minced

➢ ½ teaspoon ground cumin

➢ Salt and freshly ground black pepper to taste

➢ 4 large bell peppers, tops cut off, seeds and membrane removed

➢ ½ cup shredded low-fat mozzarella cheese

Directions:

1. Preheat the toaster oven to 375° F.

2. Combine the filling ingredients in a bowl and adjust the seasonings. Spoon the mixture to generously fill each pepper. Place the peppers upright in an 8½ × 8½ × 2-inch oiled or nonstick square (cake) pan.

3. BAKE for 40 minutes, or until the peppers are tender. Remove from the oven and sprinkle the cheese in equal portions on top of the peppers.

4. BROIL 5 minutes, or until the cheese is melted.

Garlic-lemon Shrimp Skewers

Servings: 2

Cooking Time: 8 Minutes

Ingredients:

- Juice and zest of 1 lemon
- 1 tablespoon olive oil
- ½ teaspoon garlic puree
- ¼ teaspoon smoked paprika
- 12 large shrimp, peeled and deveined
- Oil spray (hand-pumped)
- Sea salt, for seasoning
- Freshly ground black pepper, for seasoning
- 1 tablespoon chopped fresh parsley

Directions:

1. Preheat the toaster oven to 350°F on AIR FRY for 5 minutes.
2. In a medium bowl, stir the lemon juice, lemon zest, olive oil, garlic, and paprika.
3. Add the shrimp and toss to combine. Cover, refrigerate, and let marinate for 30 minutes.
4. Soak 4 wooden skewers in water while the shrimp marinate.
5. Place the air-fryer basket in the baking tray and spray it generously with the oil.
6. Thread 3 shrimp on each skewer and place them in the basket. Discard any remaining marinade.
7. In position 2, air fry for 8 minutes, turning halfway through, until just cooked.
8. Season with the salt and pepper and serve topped with the parsley.

Sesame-crusted Tuna Steaks

Servings: 3

Cooking Time: 13 Minutes

Ingredients:

- ½ cup Sesame seeds, preferably a blend of white and black
- 1½ tablespoons Toasted sesame oil
- 3 6-ounce skinless tuna steaks

Directions:

1. Preheat the toaster oven to 400°F.

2. Pour the sesame seeds on a dinner plate. Use ½ tablespoon of the sesame oil as a rub on both sides and the edges of a tuna steak. Set it in the sesame seeds, then turn it several times, pressing gently, to create an even coating of the seeds, including around the steak's edge. Set aside and continue coating the remaining steak(s).

3. When the machine is at temperature, set the steaks in the air fryer oven with as much air space between them as possible. Air-fry undisturbed for 10 minutes for medium-rare (not USDA-approved), or 12 to 13 minutes for cooked through (USDA-approved).

4. Use a nonstick-safe spatula to transfer the steaks to serving plates. Serve hot.

Shrimp With Jalapeño Dip

Servings: 4

Cooking Time: 10 Minutes

Ingredients:

- ➢ Seasonings:
- ➢ 1 teaspoon ground cumin
- ➢ 1 tablespoon minced garlic
- ➢ 1 teaspoon paprika
- ➢ 1 teaspoon chili powder
- ➢ Pinch of cayenne
- ➢ Salt to taste
- ➢ 1½ pounds large shrimp, peeled and deveined

Directions:

1. Combine the seasonings in a plastic bag, add the shrimp, and shake well to coat. Transfer the shrimp to an oiled or nonstick 8½ × 8½ × 2-inch square baking (cake) pan.

2. BROIL for 5 minutes. Remove the pan from the oven and turn the shrimp with tongs. Broil 5 minutes again, or until the shrimp are cooked (they should be firm but not rubbery.) Serve with Jalapeño Dip.

Shrimp, Chorizo And Fingerling Potatoes

Servings: 4

Cooking Time: 16 Minutes

Ingredients:

- ½ red onion, chopped into 1-inch chunks
- 8 fingerling potatoes, sliced into 1-inch slices or halved lengthwise
- 1 teaspoon olive oil
- salt and freshly ground black pepper
- 8 ounces raw chorizo sausage, sliced into 1-inch chunks
- 16 raw large shrimp, peeled, deveined and tails removed
- 1 lime
- ¼ cup chopped fresh cilantro
- chopped orange zest (optional)

Directions:

1. Preheat the toaster oven to 380°F.

2. Combine the red onion and potato chunks in a bowl and toss with the olive oil, salt and freshly ground black pepper.

3. Transfer the vegetables to the air fryer oven and air-fry for 6 minutes.

4. Add the chorizo chunks and continue to air-fry for another 5 minutes.

5. Add the shrimp, season with salt and continue to air-fry for another 5 minutes.

6. Transfer the tossed shrimp, chorizo and potato to a bowl and squeeze some lime juice over the top to taste. Toss in the fresh cilantro, orange zest and a drizzle of olive oil, and season again to taste.

7. Serve with a fresh green salad.

Sea Bass With Potato Scales And Caper Aïoli

Servings: 2

Cooking Time: 10 Minutes

Ingredients:

➢ 2 (6- to 8-ounce) fillets of sea bass

➢ salt and freshly ground black pepper

➢ ¼ cup mayonnaise

➢ 2 teaspoons finely chopped lemon zest

➢ 1 teaspoon chopped fresh thyme

➢ 2 fingerling potatoes, very thinly sliced into rounds

➢ olive oil

➢ ½ clove garlic, crushed into a paste

➢ 1 tablespoon capers, drained and rinsed

➢ 1 tablespoon olive oil

➢ 1 teaspoon lemon juice, to taste

Directions:

1. Preheat the toaster oven to 400°F.

2. Season the fish well with salt and freshly ground black pepper. Mix the mayonnaise, lemon zest and thyme together in a small bowl. Spread a thin layer of the mayonnaise mixture on both fillets. Start layering rows of potato slices onto the fish fillets to simulate the fish scales. The second row should overlap the first row slightly. Dabbing a little more mayonnaise along the upper edge of the row of potatoes where the next row overlaps will help the potato slices stick. Press the potatoes onto the fish to secure them well and season again with salt. Brush or spray the potato layer with olive oil.

3. Transfer the fish to the air fryer oven and air-fry for 8 to 10 minutes, depending on the thickness of your fillets. 1-inch of fish should take 10 minutes at 400°F.

4. While the fish is cooking, add the garlic, capers, olive oil and lemon juice to the remaining mayonnaise mixture to make the caper aïoli.

5. Serve the fish warm with a dollop of the aïoli on top or on the side.

Roasted Fish With Provençal Crumb Topping

Servings: 3

Cooking Time: 25 Minutes

Ingredients:

- 1 tablespoon olive oil, plus more for greasing
- ⅓ cup finely chopped onion
- 1 clove garlic, minced
- ¾ cup fresh bread crumbs
- 2 tablespoons chopped fresh flat-leaf (Italian) parsley
- 1 teaspoon fresh thyme leaves
- 3 (5-ounce) cod fillets, or other white-fleshed, mild-flavored fish, patted dry (about 1 ¼ inches thick)
- 2 tablespoons dry white wine
- 2 teaspoons fresh lemon juice

Directions:

1. Preheat the toaster oven to 400°F. Lightly grease the baking pan with olive oil.

2. Heat the tablespoon of olive oil in a small skillet over medium-high heat. Add the onion and cook, stirring frequently, for 3 to 4 minutes, or until tender. Add the garlic and cook for 30 seconds. Remove the skillet from the heat. Stir in the bread crumbs, parsley, and thyme.

3. Place the fish in the prepared pan. Drizzle with the wine. Divide the crumb mixture evenly over the top of each fish fillet, and press onto the fillets. Roast for 20 to 25 minutes, or until the top is brown and the fish is opaque and flakes easily when tested with a fork. Sprinkle the lemon juice evenly over the fish.

Coconut-crusted Shrimp

Servings: 4

Cooking Time: 20 Minutes

Ingredients:

- ➢ Oil spray (hand-pumped)
- ➢ ½ cup all-purpose flour
- ➢ 2 large eggs
- ➢ ¾ cup unsweetened, shredded coconut
- ➢ ½ cup panko bread crumbs
- ➢ ¼ teaspoon sea salt
- ➢ 1 pound (26 to 30 count) raw extra-large shrimp, peeled and deveined with tails attached

Directions:

1. Preheat the toaster oven to 400°F on AIR FRY for 5 minutes.
2. Place the air-fryer basket in the baking tray and spray it generously with the oil.
3. Place the flour on a plate and set it on your work surface.
4. In a small bowl, whisk the eggs until well beaten and place next to the flour.
5. In a medium bowl, stir the coconut, bread crumbs, and salt, and place next to the eggs.
6. Pat the shrimp dry with paper towels. Working in two batches, dredge the shrimp in the flour, then egg, then coconut mixture, and place them in the basket. Do not crowd the basket.
7. Lightly spray the shrimp with the oil on both sides and in position 2, air fry for 10 minutes, turning halfway through, until golden brown.
8. Repeat with the remaining shrimp, covering the cooked shrimp loosely with foil to keep them warm. Serve.

Roasted Pepper Tilapia

Servings: 6

Cooking Time: 20 Minutes

Ingredients:

- 6 5-ounce tilapia fillets
- 2 tablespoons olive oil
- Filling:
- 1 cucumber, peeled, seeds scooped out and discarded, and chopped
- ½ cup chopped roasted peppers, drained
- 2 tablespoons lemon juice
- 2 tablespoons chopped fresh parsley or cilantro
- 1 teaspoon garlic powder
- 1 teaspoon paprika
- Salt and freshly ground black pepper to taste
- Dip mixture:
- 1 cup nonfat sour cream
- 2 tablespoons low-fat mayonnaise
- 3 tablespoons Dijon mustard
- 1 teaspoon Worcestershire sauce
- 1 teaspoon dried dill

Directions:

1. Combine the filling ingredients in a bowl, adjusting the seasonings to taste.

2. Spoon equal portions of filling in the centers of the tilapia filets. Roll up the fillets, starting at the smallest end. Secure each roll with toothpicks and place the rolls in an oiled or nonstick baking pan. Carefully brush the fillets with oil and place them in an oiled or nonstick 8½ × 8½ × 2-inch square baking (cake) pan.

3. BROIL for 20 minutes, or until the fillets are lightly browned. Combine the dip mixture ingredients in a small bowl and serve with the fish.

Oysters Broiled In Wine Sauce

Servings: 2

Cooking Time: 20 Minutes

Ingredients:

➢ Sauce:

➢ 2 tablespoons margarine, at room temperature

➢ 1 cup dry white wine

➢ 3 garlic cloves, minced

➢ Salt and freshly ground black pepper to taste

➢ 24 fresh oysters, shucked and drained

Directions:

1. Combine the sauce ingredients in a 1-quart 8½ × 8½ × 4-inch ovenproof baking dish and adjust the seasonings to taste.

2. BROIL the sauce for 5 minutes, remove the pan from the oven, and stir. Return to the oven and broil for another 5 minutes, or until the sauce begins to bubble. Remove from the oven and cool for 5 minutes. Add the oysters, spooning the sauce over them to cover thoroughly.

3. BROIL for 5 minutes, or until the oysters are just cooked.

Catfish Kebabs

Servings: 4

Cooking Time: 20 Minutes

Ingredients:

➤ Marinade:

➤ 3 tablespoons lemon juice

➤ 3 tablespoons tomato juice

➤ 2 garlic cloves, minced

➤ 2 tablespoons olive oil

➤ 1 teaspoon soy sauce

➤ 4 5-ounce catfish fillets

➤ 4 9-inch metal skewers

➤ 2 plum tomatoes, quartered

➤ 1 onion, cut into 1 × 1-inch pieces

Directions:

1. Combine the marinade ingredients in a small bowl. Set aside.

2. Cut the fillets into 2 by 3-inch strips and place in a shallow glass or ceramic dish. Add the marinade and refrigerate, covered, for at least 20 minutes. Remove the strips from the marinade, roll, and skewer, alternating the rolled strips with the tomatoes and onion.

3. Brush the kebabs with marinade, reserving the remaining marinade for brushing again later. Place the skewers on a broiling rack with a pan underneath.

4. Broil for 10 minutes, then remove the pan from the oven and carefully turn the skewers. Brush the kebabs with the marinade and broil again for 10 minutes, or until browned.

Spiced Sea Bass

Servings: 4

Cooking Time: 25 Minutes

Ingredients:

- ➤ Brushing mixture:
- ➤ 2 tablespoons lemon juice
- ➤ 1 tablespoon chopped fresh parsley
- ➤ 2 garlic cloves, minced
- ➤ 2 6-ounce sea bass fillets, approximately 1 inch thick
- ➤ Spice mixture:
- ➤ 2 teaspoons paprika
- ➤ 2 teaspoons ground cumin
- ➤ 1 teaspoon allspice
- ➤ 2 teaspoons garlic powder
- ➤ Pinch of cayenne
- ➤ Salt to taste

Directions:

1. Combine the brushing mixture ingredients in a small bowl, mixing well. Place the fillets on a plate or platter.

2. Brush the fillets on both sides with the brushing mixture. Let stand at room temperature for 10 minutes.

3. Combine the spice mixture ingredients in a small bowl, mixing well. Transfer to a plate and press the fillets into the spice mixture to coat well. Transfer the fillets to an oiled or nonstick 8½ × 8½ × 2-inch square baking (cake) pan.

4. BROIL for 15 minutes, or until the fish flakes easily with a fork.

SNACKS APPETIZERS AND SIDES

Pizza Bagel Bites

Servings: 2

Cooking Time: 5 Minutes

Ingredients:

- ➤ 2 Mini bagel(s), split into two rings
- ➤ ¼ cup Purchased pizza sauce
- ➤ ½ cup Finely grated or shredded cheese, such as Parmesan cheese, semi-firm mozzarella, fontina, or (preferably) a cheese blend

Directions:

1. Preheat the toaster oven to 375°F .

2. Spread the cut side of each bagel half with 1 tablespoon pizza sauce; top each half with 2 tablespoons shredded cheese.

3. When the machine is at temperature, put the bagels cheese side up in the air fryer oven in one layer. Air-fry undisturbed for 4 minutes, or until the cheese has melted and is gooey. You may need to air-fry the pizza bagel bites for 1 minute extra if the temperature is at 360°F.

4. Use a nonstick-safe spatula to transfer the topped bagel halves to a wire rack. Cool for at least 5 minutes before serving.

Baked Asparagus Fries

Servings: 2-3

Cooking Time: 14 Minutes

Ingredients:

- 1 1/2 cups mayonnaise
- 3/4 cup grated Parmesan cheese
- 2 cloves garlic, minced
- 1 tablespoon dried parsley
- 1 tablespoon Italian seasoning
- 1 teaspoon salt
- 1/2 teaspoon coarse black pepper
- 1/2 pound thick asparagus, trimmed
- 1 cup panko crumbs

Directions:

1. Heat the oven to 425ºF.

2. In a small bowl, combine mayonnaise, Parmesan cheese, garlic, parsley, Italian seasoning, salt and black pepper.

3. Brush asparagus with 3 tablespoons mayonnaise mixture and roll in crumbs. Place asparagus on the baking pan.

4. Bake 12 to 14 minutes or until lightly browned and asparagus are cooked.

5. Serve asparagus with the remaining mayonnaise mixture.

Rosemary Roasted Vegetables

Servings: 4

Cooking Time: 25 Minutes

Ingredients:

- ➢ 3 tablespoons olive oil
- ➢ Grated zest and juice of 1 lemon
- ➢ 2 tablespoons chopped fresh rosemary leaves
- ➢ 4 cloves garlic, minced
- ➢ Kosher salt and freshly ground black pepper
- ➢ 6 cups vegetables, diced, such as bell peppers, onions, zucchini, mushrooms, cherry tomatoes, potatoes, and eggplant

Directions:

1. Preheat the toaster oven to 425 °F.
2. Stir the olive oil, lemon zest, lemon juice, rosemary, and garlic in a small bowl. Season with salt and pepper. Place the vegetables into a large bowl and drizzle the olive oil mixture over all. Stir gently to coat.
3. Arrange the vegetables in a single layer in a 12 x 12-inch baking pan. Roast for 10 minutes. Stir and roast for an additional 10 to 15 minutes, or until the vegetables are tender.

Wonton Cups

Servings: 6

Cooking Time: 10 Minutes

Ingredients:

- 6 wonton wrappers (3-inch squares)
- 2 Tablespoons melted butter
- Filling of choice

Directions:

1. Preheat toaster oven to 350°F.
2. Carefully press and fold one wonton wrapper in each cup of a 6-cup muffin pan.
3. Very lightly brush edges of wrappers with butter.
4. Bake 8 to 10 minutes or until golden brown.

Baked Coconut Shrimp With Curried Chutney

Servings: 8-10

Cooking Time: 11 Minutes

Ingredients:

- 1 cup chutney
- 2 Tablespoons sliced green onion
- 1/2 teaspoon ground curry
- 1/2 teaspoon crushed red pepper
- 2 Tablespoons all-purpose flour
- 1 teaspoon salt
- 1 cup panko breadcrumbs
- 3/4 cup sweetened shredded coconut
- 1 egg white
- 1 pound (16 to 20 count) extra jumbo shrimp
- Cilantro

Directions:

1. In a small bowl, stir chutney, green onion, curry and crushed red pepper until blended. Set aside.
2. Preheat the toaster oven to 450°F. Spray a baking pan with nonstick cooking spray. Set aside.
3. In a large resealable plastic bag, combine flour and salt.
4. Add panko breadcrumbs and coconut to bag. Seal and shake to combine.
5. In a medium bowl, whisk egg white until foamy.
6. Dip one shrimp at a time into egg white.
7. Place shrimp in crumb mixture and press mixture onto shrimp until well coated. Arrange in single layer in prepared baking pan.
8. Bake for 9 to 11 minutes or until crumbs are golden brown. Serve with chutney mixture. Garnish with cilantro.

Simple Holiday Stuffing

Servings: 4

Cooking Time: 120 Minutes

Ingredients:

- 12 ounces hearty white sandwich bread, cut into ½-inch pieces (8 cups)
- 1 onion, chopped fine
- 1 celery rib, chopped fine
- 1 tablespoon unsalted butter, plus 5 tablespoons, melted
- 1 tablespoon minced fresh thyme or 1 teaspoon dried
- 2 teaspoons minced fresh sage or ½ teaspoon dried
- ¾ teaspoon table salt
- ¼ teaspoon pepper
- 1¼ cups chicken broth

Directions:

1. Adjust toaster oven rack to middle position and preheat the toaster oven to 300 degrees. Spread bread into even layer on small rimmed baking sheet and bake until light golden brown, 35 to 45 minutes, tossing halfway through baking. Let bread cool completely on sheet.

2. Increase oven temperature to 375 degrees. Microwave onion, celery, 1 tablespoon butter, thyme, sage, salt, and pepper in covered large bowl, stirring occasionally, until vegetables are softened, 2 to 4 minutes.

3. Stir in broth, then add bread and toss to combine. Let mixture sit for 10 minutes, then toss mixture again until broth is fully absorbed. Transfer bread mixture to 8-inch square baking dish or pan and distribute evenly but do not pack down. (Stuffing can be covered and refrigerated for up to 24 hours; increase covered baking time to 15 minutes.)

4. Drizzle melted butter evenly over top of stuffing. Cover dish tightly with aluminum foil and bake for 10 minutes. Uncover and continue to bake until top is golden brown and crisp, 15 to 25 minutes. Transfer dish to wire rack and let cool for 10 minutes. Serve.

Garden Fresh Bruschetta

Servings: 6

Cooking Time: 5 Minutes

Ingredients:

- 1/2 cup Parmigiano-Reggiano cheese
- 2 cloves garlic (or to taste)
- 2 tablespoons balsamic vinegar
- 1/3 cup pine nuts
- 1 loaf crusty Italian bread
- 1 or 2 fresh tomatoes, sliced or chopped
- Salt and pepper to taste
- 4 cups fresh basil leaves, stems removed

Directions:

1. With shredding disk inserted, shred cheese in food processor. Remove from food processor and set aside.

2. Insert S-blade in food processor and coarsely chop basil leaves and garlic. Add vinegar and pulse a few times. Add pine nuts to basil mixture and pulse until coarsely chopped. With food processor running, drizzle olive oil through feed chute until ingredients are coated and spreadable. Add half of the already grated Parmesan cheese and pulse until just blended.

3. To assemble: Slice crusty bread on diagonal, place on toaster oven size cookie sheet. On each piece of bread, spread basil mixture. Place tomatoes on top of basil, add salt and pepper to taste. Sprinkle some of the remaining cheese on top.

4. Place in preheated 350°F toaster oven for 5 minutes or until cheese melts and bread is warmed. Serve as an appetizer.

Cajun Roasted Okra

Servings: 4-6

Cooking Time: 40 Minutes

Ingredients:

- ➢ 1 pound okra, tops removed and sliced in half lengthwise
- ➢ 2 Tablespoons olive oil
- ➢ 1 teaspoon Cajun seasoning
- ➢ 1/2 teaspoon black pepper
- ➢ Sea salt to taste
- ➢ Cajun Dipping Sauce

Directions:

1. Preheat the toaster oven to 450°F.
2. Line a 15X9X1-inch baking pan with aluminum foil and spray with nonstick cooking spray.
3. Place okra, olive oil, Cajun seasoning, pepper and salt in prepared pan; stir until well coated.
4. Bake 35 to 40 minutes or until okra is crisp.
5. Serve with Cajun Dipping Sauce.

Cheese Arancini

Servings: 8

Cooking Time: 12 Minutes

Ingredients:

- 1 cup Water
- ½ cup Raw white Arborio rice
- 1½ teaspoons Butter
- ¼ teaspoon Table salt
- 8 ¾-inch semi-firm mozzarella cubes (not fresh mozzarella)
- 2 Large egg(s), well beaten
- 1 cup Seasoned Italian-style dried bread crumbs (gluten-free, if a concern)
- Olive oil spray

Directions:

1. Combine the water, rice, butter, and salt in a small saucepan. Bring to a boil over medium-high heat, stirring occasionally. Cover, reduce the heat to very low, and simmer very slowly for 20 minutes.

2. Take the saucepan off the heat and let it stand, covered, for 10 minutes. Uncover it and fluff the rice. Cool for 20 minutes. (The rice can be made up to 1 hour in advance; keep it covered in its saucepan.)

3. Preheat the toaster oven to 375°F .

4. Set up and fill two shallow soup plates or small bowls on your counter: one with the beaten egg(s) and one with the bread crumbs.

5. With clean but wet hands, scoop up about 2 tablespoons of the cooked rice and form it into a ball. Push a cube of mozzarella into the middle of the ball and seal the cheese inside. Dip the ball in the egg(s) to coat completely, letting any excess egg slip back into the rest. Roll the ball in the bread crumbs to coat evenly but lightly. Set aside and continue making more rice balls.

6. Generously spray the balls with olive oil spray, then set them in the air fryer oven in one layer. They must not touch. Air-fry undisturbed for 10 minutes, or until crunchy and golden brown. If the machine is at 360°F, you may need to add 2 minutes to the cooking time.

7. Use a nonstick-safe spatula, and maybe a flatware spoon for balance, to gently transfer the balls to a wire rack. Cool for at least 5 minutes or up to 20 minutes before serving.

Stuffed Mushrooms

Servings: 10

Cooking Time: 8 Minutes

Ingredients:

- 8 ounces white mushroom caps, stems removed
- salt
- 6 fresh mozzarella cheese balls
- ground dried thyme
- ¼ roasted red pepper cut into small pieces (about ½ inch)

Directions:

1. Sprinkle inside of mushroom caps with salt to taste.
2. Cut mozzarella balls in half.
3. Stuff each cap with half a mozzarella cheese ball. Sprinkle very lightly with thyme.
4. Top each mushroom with a small strip of roasted red pepper, lightly pressing it into the cheese.
5. Air-fry at 390°F for 8 minutes or longer if you prefer softer mushrooms.

Asparagus With Pistachio Dukkah

Servings: 3   Cooking Time: 8 Minutes

Ingredients:

- Pistachio Dukkah Ingredients
- 3 tablespoons coriander seeds
- 1 tablespoon cumin seeds
- ½ cup shelled pistachios
- ¼ cup sesame seeds
- 1 teaspoon salt
- ½ teaspoon pepper
- Asparagus Ingredients
- 1 bundle asparagus spears
- 1 tablespoon olive oil
- Salt & pepper, to taste

Directions:

1. Make the pistachio dukkah by placing the coriander and cumin seeds in a skillet over medium heat. Toast for 2 minutes, or until fragrant. Transfer spices to a spice grinder or mortar and pestle. Allow spices to cool completely, then grind.

2. Toast the pistachios in a skillet for 5 minutes, or until golden brown and fragrant. Transfer to a cutting board and chop finely. Add the sesame seeds to the same skillet and toast for 2 minutes, or until golden brown and

3. fragrant. Transfer the pistachios, sesame seeds, coriander, and cumin seeds to a bowl. Add salt and pepper, then stir to combine.

4. Select the Preheat function on the Cosori Smart Air Fryer Toaster Oven, adjust temperature to 430°F, and press Start/Pause.

5. Line the food tray with foil, then place the asparagus on the tray. Drizzle with olive oil and season with salt and pepper.

6. Insert food tray at top position in the preheated oven.

7. Select the Air Fry function, adjust time to 8 minutes, and press Start/Pause.

8. Remove when asparagus is tender. Place asparagus on a serving dish and sprinkle with pistachio dukkah.

9. Pistachio dukkah can be stored at room temperature in a sealed jar or container for up to 4 weeks.

Roasted Fennel With Wine + Parmesan

Servings: 3

Cooking Time: 26 Minutes

Ingredients:

- 3 medium fennel bulbs, trimmed, cored, and cut horizontally into ⅓-inch-thick slices, reserving 2 teaspoons fronds (leaves)
- 2 ½ tablespoons olive oil, plus more for greasing
- Kosher salt and freshly ground black pepper
- 2 tablespoons dry white wine
- 3 tablespoons shredded Parmesan cheese

Directions:

1. Preheat the toaster oven to 425 °F. Lightly oil a 12 x 12-inch baking pan.

2. Arrange the fennel in a single layer on the prepared pan. Drizzle the olive oil evenly over and season with salt and pepper. Stir to blend well and arrange in a single layer. Roast for 12 minutes. Stir and roast for an additional 10 to 12 minutes, or until the fennel is brown and crisp around the edges and the largest piece is tender when pierced with the tip of a knife.

3. Carefully remove the pan from the oven. Drizzle the wine over the cooked fennel and sprinkle with the Parmesan cheese. Return to the oven and bake for an additional 2 minutes or until the cheese is melted. Sprinkle with the reserved fronds before serving warm.

Brazilian Cheese Bread (pão De Queijo)

Servings: 8

Cooking Time: 18 Minutes

Ingredients:

- ➢ 1 large egg, room temperature
- ➢ ⅓ cup olive oil
- ➢ ⅔ cups whole milk 1½ cups tapioca flour
- ➢ ½ cup feta cheese
- ➢ ¼ cup Parmesan cheese
- ➢ 1 teaspoon kosher salt
- ➢ ¼ teaspoon garlic powder
- ➢ Cooking spray

Directions:

1. Blend the egg, olive oil, milk, tapioca flour, feta, Parmesan, salt, and garlic powder in a stand mixer until smooth.
2. Spray the mini muffin pan with cooking spray.
3. Pour the batter into the muffin cups so they are ¾ full.
4. .Preheat the toaster oven to 380°F.
5. Place the muffin pan on the wire rack, then insert rack at mid position in the preheated oven.
6. Select the Bake function, adjust time to 18 minutes, and press Start/Pause.
7. Remove when done, then carefully pop the bread from the mini muffin tin and serve.

POULTRY

Crispy Fried Onion Chicken Breasts

Servings: 2

Cooking Time: 13 Minutes

Ingredients:

- ¼ cup all-purpose flour
- salt and freshly ground black pepper
- 1 egg
- 2 tablespoons Dijon mustard
- 1½ cups crispy fried onions (like French's®)
- ½ teaspoon paprika
- 2 (5-ounce) boneless, skinless chicken breasts
- vegetable or olive oil, in a spray bottle

Directions:

1. Preheat the toaster oven to 380°F.

2. Set up a dredging station with three shallow dishes. Place the flour in the first shallow dish and season well with salt and freshly ground black pepper. Combine the egg and Dijon mustard in a second shallow dish and whisk until smooth. Place the fried onions in a sealed bag and using a rolling pin, crush them into coarse crumbs. Combine these crumbs with the paprika in the third shallow dish.

3. Dredge the chicken breasts in the flour. Shake off any excess flour and dip them into the egg mixture. Let any excess egg drip off. Then coat both sides of the chicken breasts with the crispy onions. Press the crumbs onto the chicken breasts with your hands to make sure they are well adhered.

4. Spray or brush the bottom of the air fryer oven with oil. Transfer the chicken breasts to the air fryer oven and air-fry at 380°F for 13 minutes, turning the chicken over halfway through the cooking time.

5. Serve immediately.

Pickle Brined Fried Chicken

Servings: 4

Cooking Time: 47 Minutes

Ingredients:

- 4 bone-in, skin-on chicken legs, cut into drumsticks and thighs (about 3½ pounds)
- pickle juice from a 24-ounce jar of kosher dill pickles
- ½ cup flour
- salt and freshly ground black pepper
- 2 eggs
- 1 cup fine breadcrumbs
- 1 teaspoon salt
- 1 teaspoon freshly ground black pepper
- ½ teaspoon ground paprika
- ⅛ teaspoon ground cayenne pepper
- vegetable or canola oil in a spray bottle

Directions:

1. Place the chicken in a shallow dish and pour the pickle juice over the top. Cover and transfer the chicken to the refrigerator to brine in the pickle juice for 3 to 8 hours.

2. When you are ready to cook, remove the chicken from the refrigerator to let it come to room temperature while you set up a dredging station. Place the flour in a shallow dish and season well with salt and freshly ground black pepper. Whisk the eggs in a second shallow dish. In a third shallow dish, combine the breadcrumbs, salt, pepper, paprika and cayenne pepper.

3. Preheat the toaster oven to 370°F.

4. Remove the chicken from the pickle brine and gently dry it with a clean kitchen towel. Dredge each piece of chicken in the flour, then dip it into the egg mixture, and finally press it into the breadcrumb mixture to coat all sides of the chicken. Place the breaded chicken on a plate or baking sheet and spray each piece all over with vegetable oil.

5. Air-fry the chicken in two batches. Place two chicken thighs and two drumsticks into the air fryer oven. Air-fry for 10 minutes. Then, gently turn the chicken pieces over and air-fry for another 10 minutes. Remove the chicken pieces and let them rest on plate – do not cover. Repeat with the second batch of chicken, air-frying for 20 minutes, turning the chicken over halfway through.

6. Lower the temperature of the air fryer oven to 340°F. Place the first batch of chicken on top of the second batch already in the air fryer oven and air-fry for an additional 7 minutes. Serve warm and enjoy.

Sweet-and-sour Chicken

Servings: 6 | Cooking Time: 10 Minutes

Ingredients:

- 1 cup pineapple juice
- 1 cup plus 3 tablespoons cornstarch, divided
- ¼ cup sugar
- ¼ cup ketchup
- ¼ cup apple cider vinegar
- 2 tablespoons soy sauce or tamari
- 1 teaspoon garlic powder, divided
- ¼ cup flour
- 1 tablespoon sesame seeds
- ½ teaspoon salt
- ¼ teaspoon ground black pepper
- 2 large eggs
- 2 pounds chicken breasts, cut into 1-inch cubes
- 1 red bell pepper, cut into 1-inch pieces
- 1 carrot, sliced into ¼-inch-thick rounds

Directions:

1. In a medium saucepan, whisk together the pineapple juice, 3 tablespoons of the cornstarch, the sugar, the ketchup, the apple cider vinegar, the soy sauce or tamari, and ½ teaspoon of the garlic powder. Cook over medium-low heat, whisking occasionally as the sauce thickens, about 6 minutes. Stir and set aside while preparing the chicken.

2. Preheat the toaster oven to 370°F.

3. In a medium bowl, place the remaining 1 cup of cornstarch, the flour, the sesame seeds, the salt, the remaining ½ teaspoon of garlic powder, and the pepper.

4. In a second medium bowl, whisk the eggs.

5. Working in batches, place the cubed chicken in the cornstarch mixture to lightly coat; then dip it into the egg mixture, and return it to the cornstarch mixture. Shake off the excess and place the coated chicken in the air fryer oven. Spray with cooking spray and air-fry for 5 minutes, and spray with more cooking spray. Cook an additional 3 to 5 minutes, or until completely cooked and golden brown.

6. On the last batch of chicken, add the bell pepper and carrot to the air fryer oven and cook with the chicken.

7. Place the cooked chicken and vegetables into a serving bowl and toss with the sweet-and-sour sauce to serve.

Chicken-fried Steak With Gravy

Servings: 2   Cooking Time: 16 Minutes

Ingredients:

- FOR THE STEAK
- Oil spray (hand-pumped)
- 1 cup all-purpose flour
- 1 teaspoon garlic powder
- 1 teaspoon onion powder
- 1 teaspoon smoked paprika
- 2 large eggs
- 2 (½-pound) cube steaks
- Sea salt, for seasoning
- Freshly ground black pepper, for seasoning
- FOR THE GRAVY
- 2 tablespoons salted butter
- 2 tablespoons all-purpose flour
- 1½ cups whole milk
- ¼ cup heavy (whipping) cream
- Sea salt, for seasoning
- Freshly ground black pepper, for seasoning

Directions:

1. To make the steak
2. Preheat the toaster oven to 400°F on AIR FRY for 5 minutes.
3. Place the air-fryer basket in the baking tray and spray it generously with the oil.
4. In a medium bowl, stir the flour, garlic powder, onion powder, and paprika until well blended.
5. In a medium bowl, beat the eggs and place them next to the flour.
6. Season the steaks all over with salt and pepper.
7. Dredge a steak in the egg and then in the flour mixture, making sure it is well coated. Shake off any excess flour.
8. Place the steak in the basket and repeat the process with the other steak.
9. Spray the tops of the steaks with the oil.
10. In position 2, air fry for 9 minutes until golden brown and crispy. Turn the steaks over, spray the second side with the oil, and air fry for an additional 7 minutes.
11. Set the steaks aside to rest for 5 minutes.
12. To make the gravy
13. While the steak is air frying, melt the butter in a medium saucepan over medium-high heat.
14. Whisk in the flour and cook for 2 minutes until lightly browned.
15. Whisk in the milk until the gravy is creamy and thick, about 5 minutes. Whisk in the cream and season with salt and pepper.
16. Serve the steak topped with the gravy.

Chicken Wellington

| Servings: 4 | Cooking Time: 30 Minutes |

Ingredients:

- ➢ 2 small (5- to 6-ounce) boneless, skinless chicken breast halves
- ➢ Kosher salt and freshly ground black pepper
- ➢ 2 teaspoons Italian seasoning
- ➢ 2 tablespoons olive oil
- ➢ 3 tablespoons unsalted butter, softened
- ➢ 3 ounces cream cheese, softened (about ⅓ cup)
- ➢ ¾ cup shredded Monterey Jack cheese
- ➢ ¼ cup grated Parmesan cheese
- ➢ 1 cup frozen (loose-pack) chopped spinach, thawed and squeezed dry
- ➢ ¾ cup chopped canned artichoke hearts, drained
- ➢ ½ teaspoon garlic powder
- ➢ 1 sheet frozen puff pastry, about 9 inches square, thawed (½ of a 17.3-ounce package)
- ➢ 1 large egg, lightly beaten

Directions:

1. Preheat the toaster oven to 425° F. Line a 12 x 12-inch baking pan with parchment paper.

2. Cut the chicken breasts in half lengthwise. Season each piece with the salt, pepper, and Italian seasoning. Fold the thinner end under the larger piece to make the chicken breasts into a rounded shape. Secure with toothpicks.

3. Heat a large skillet over medium-high heat. Add the olive oil and heat. Add the chicken breasts and brown well, turning to brown evenly. Remove from the skillet and set aside to cool. Remove the toothpicks.

4. Stir the butter, cream cheese, Monterey Jack, and Parmesan in a large bowl. Stir in the spinach, artichoke hearts, and garlic powder. Season with salt and pepper.

5. Roll out the puff pastry sheet on a lightly floured board until it makes a 12-inch square. Cut into four equal pieces. Spread one-fourth of the spinach-artichoke mixture on the surface of each pastry square to within ½ inch of all four edges. Place the chicken in the center of each. Gently fold the puff pastry up over the chicken and pinch the edges to seal tightly.

6. Place each chicken bundle, seam side down, on the prepared pan. Brush the top of each bundle lightly with the beaten egg. Bake for 25 to 30 minutes, or until the pastry is golden brown and crisp and a meat thermometer inserted into the chicken reaches 165°F.

Orange-glazed Roast Chicken

Servings: 6

Cooking Time: 100 Minutes

Ingredients:

- 1 3-pound whole chicken, rinsed and patted dry with paper towels
- Brushing mixture:
- 2 tablespoons orange juice concentrate
- 1 tablespoon soy sauce
- 1 tablespoon toasted sesame oil
- 1 teaspoon ground ginger
- Salt and freshly ground black pepper to taste

Directions:

1. Preheat the toaster oven to 400° F.

2. Place the chicken, breast side up, in an oiled or nonstick 8½ × 8½ × 2-inch square (cake) pan and brush with the mixture, which has been combined in a small bowl, reserving the remaining mixture. Cover with aluminum foil.

3. BAKE for 1 hour and 20 minutes. Uncover and brush the chicken with remaining mixture.

4. BAKE, uncovered, for 20 minutes, or until the breast is tender when pierced with a fork and golden brown.

Fried Chicken

Servings: 4   Cooking Time: 40 Minutes

Ingredients:

- 12 skin-on chicken drumsticks
- 1 cup buttermilk
- 1½ cups all-purpose flour
- 1 tablespoon smoked paprika
- ¾ teaspoon celery salt
- ¾ teaspoon dried mustard
- ½ teaspoon garlic powder
- ½ teaspoon freshly ground black pepper
- ½ teaspoon sea salt
- ½ teaspoon dried thyme
- ¼ teaspoon dried oregano
- 4 large eggs
- Oil spray (hand-pumped)

Directions:

1. Place the chicken and buttermilk in a medium bowl, cover, and refrigerate for at least 1 hour, up to overnight.

2. Preheat the toaster oven to 375°F on AIR FRY for 5 minutes.

3. In a large bowl, stir the flour, paprika, celery salt, mustard, garlic powder, pepper, salt, thyme, and oregano until well mixed.

4. Beat the eggs until frothy in a medium bowl and set them beside the flour.

5. Place the air-fryer basket in the baking tray and generously spray it with the oil.

6. Dredge a chicken drumstick in the flour, then the eggs, and then in the flour again, thickly coating it, and place the drumstick in the basket. Repeat with 5 more drumsticks and spray them all lightly with the oil on all sides.

7. In position 2, air fry for 20 minutes, turning halfway through, until golden brown and crispy with an internal temperature of 165°F.

8. Repeat with the remaining chicken, covering the cooked chicken loosely with foil to keep it warm. Serve.

Jerk Turkey Meatballs

Servings: 7

Cooking Time: 8 Minutes

Ingredients:

- 1 pound lean ground turkey
- ¼ cup chopped onion
- 1 teaspoon minced garlic
- ½ teaspoon dried thyme
- ¼ teaspoon ground cinnamon
- 1 teaspoon cayenne pepper
- ½ teaspoon paprika
- ½ teaspoon salt
- ⅛ teaspoon black pepper
- ¼ teaspoon red pepper flakes
- 2 teaspoons brown sugar
- 1 large egg, whisked
- ⅓ cup panko breadcrumbs
- 2⅓ cups cooked brown Jasmine rice
- 2 green onions, chopped
- ¾ cup sweet onion dressing

Directions:

1. Preheat the toaster oven to 350°F.

2. In a medium bowl, mix the ground turkey with the onion, garlic, thyme, cinnamon, cayenne pepper, paprika, salt, pepper, red pepper flakes, and brown sugar. Add the whisked egg and stir in the breadcrumbs until the turkey starts to hold together.

3. Using a 1-ounce scoop, portion the turkey into meatballs. You should get about 28 meatballs.

4. Spray the air fryer oven with olive oil spray.

5. Place the meatballs into the air fryer oven and air-fry for 5 minutes, rotate the meatball, and cook another 2 to 4 minutes (or until the internal temperature of the meatballs reaches 165°F).

6. Remove the meatballs from the air fryer oven and repeat for the remaining meatballs.

7. Serve warm over a bed of rice with chopped green onions and spicy Caribbean jerk dressing.

Harissa Lemon Whole Chicken

Servings: 6

Cooking Time: 60 Minutes

Ingredients:

- 2 teaspoons kosher salt
- ½ teaspoon freshly ground black pepper
- ½ teaspoon ground cumin
- 2 garlic cloves
- 6 tablespoons harissa paste
- ½ lemon, juiced
- 1 whole lemon, zested
- 1 (5 pound) whole chicken

Directions:

1. Place salt, pepper, cumin, garlic cloves, harissa paste, lemon juice, and lemon zest in a food processor and pulse until they form a smooth puree.

2. Rub the puree all over the chicken, especially inside the cavity, and cover with plastic wrap.

3. Marinate for 1 hour at room temperature.

4. Preheat the toaster oven to 350°F.

5. Place the marinated chicken on the food tray, then insert the tray at low position in the preheated oven.

6. Select the Roast function, then press Start/Pause.

7. Remove when done, tent chicken with foil, and allow it to rest for 20 minutes before serving.

Poblano Bake

Servings: 4

Cooking Time: 11 Minutes

Ingredients:

- ➢ 2 large poblano peppers (approx. 5½ inches long excluding stem)
- ➢ ¾ pound ground turkey, raw
- ➢ ¾ cup cooked brown rice
- ➢ 1 teaspoon chile powder
- ➢ ½ teaspoon ground cumin
- ➢ ½ teaspoon garlic powder
- ➢ 4 ounces sharp Cheddar cheese, grated
- ➢ 1 8-ounce jar salsa, warmed

Directions:

1. Slice each pepper in half lengthwise so that you have four wide, flat pepper halves.
2. Remove seeds and membrane and discard. Rinse inside and out.
3. In a large bowl, combine turkey, rice, chile powder, cumin, and garlic powder. Mix well.
4. Divide turkey filling into 4 portions and stuff one into each of the 4 pepper halves. Press lightly to pack down.
5. Place 2 pepper halves in air fryer oven and air-fry at 390°F for 10 minutes or until turkey is well done.
6. Top each pepper half with ¼ of the grated cheese. Cook 1 more minute or just until cheese melts.
7. Repeat steps 5 and 6 to cook remaining pepper halves.
8. To serve, place each pepper half on a plate and top with ¼ cup warm salsa.

Sesame Orange Chicken

Servings: 2

Cooking Time: 9 Minutes

Ingredients:

- ➢ 1 pound boneless, skinless chicken breasts, cut into cubes
- ➢ salt and freshly ground black pepper
- ➢ ¼ cup cornstarch
- ➢ 2 eggs, beaten
- ➢ 1½ cups panko breadcrumbs
- ➢ vegetable or peanut oil, in a spray bottle
- ➢ 12 ounces orange marmalade
- ➢ 1 tablespoon soy sauce
- ➢ 1 teaspoon minced ginger
- ➢ 2 tablespoons hoisin sauce
- ➢ 1 tablespoon sesame oil
- ➢ sesame seeds, toasted

Directions:

1. Season the chicken pieces with salt and pepper. Set up a dredging station. Put the cornstarch in a zipper-sealable plastic bag. Place the beaten eggs in a bowl and put the panko breadcrumbs in a shallow dish. Transfer the seasoned chicken to the bag with the cornstarch and shake well to completely coat the chicken on all sides. Remove the chicken from the bag, shaking off any excess cornstarch and dip the pieces into the egg. Let any excess egg drip from the chicken and transfer into the breadcrumbs, pressing the crumbs onto the chicken pieces with your hands. Spray the chicken pieces with vegetable or peanut oil.

2. Preheat the toaster oven to 400°F.

3. Combine the orange marmalade, soy sauce, ginger, hoisin sauce and sesame oil in a saucepan. Bring the mixture to a boil on the stovetop, lower the heat and simmer for 10 minutes, until the sauce has thickened. Set aside and keep warm.

4. Transfer the coated chicken to the air fryer oven and air-fry at 400°F for 9 minutes, rotate a few times during the cooking process to help the chicken cook evenly.

5. Right before serving, toss the browned chicken pieces with the sesame orange sauce. Serve over white rice with steamed broccoli. Sprinkle the sesame seeds on top.

Tandoori Chicken Legs

Servings: 2

Cooking Time: 30 Minutes

Ingredients:

- 1 cup plain yogurt
- 2 cloves garlic, minced
- 1 tablespoon grated fresh ginger
- 2 teaspoons paprika
- 2 teaspoons ground coriander
- 1 teaspoon ground turmeric
- 1 teaspoon salt
- ¼ teaspoon ground cayenne pepper
- juice of 1 lime
- 2 bone-in, skin-on chicken legs
- fresh cilantro leaves

Directions:

1. Make the marinade by combining the yogurt, garlic, ginger, spices and lime juice. Make slashes into the chicken legs to help the marinade penetrate the meat. Pour the marinade over the chicken legs, cover and let the chicken marinate for at least an hour or overnight in the refrigerator.

2. Preheat the toaster oven oven to 380°F.

3. Transfer the chicken legs from the marinade to the air fryer oven, reserving any extra marinade. Air-fry for 15 minutes. Flip the chicken over and pour the remaining marinade over the top. Air-fry for another 15 minutes, watching to make sure it doesn't brown too much. If it does start to get too brown, you can loosely tent the chicken with aluminum foil, tucking the ends of the foil under the chicken to stop it from blowing around.

4. Serve over rice with some fresh cilantro on top.

Italian Roasted Chicken Thighs

Servings: 6

Cooking Time: 14 Minutes

Ingredients:

- 6 boneless chicken thighs
- ½ teaspoon dried oregano
- ½ teaspoon garlic powder
- ½ teaspoon sea salt
- ½ teaspoon black pepper
- ¼ teaspoon crushed red pepper flakes

Directions:

1. Pat the chicken thighs with paper towel.
2. In a small bowl, mix the oregano, garlic powder, salt, pepper, and crushed red pepper flakes. Rub the spice mixture onto the chicken thighs.
3. Preheat the toaster oven to 400°F.
4. Place the chicken thighs in the air fryer oven and spray with cooking spray. Air-fry for 10 minutes, turn over, and cook another 4 minutes. When cooking completes, the internal temperature should read 165°F.

BEEF PORK AND LAMB

Extra Crispy Country-style Pork Riblets

Servings: 3

Cooking Time: 30 Minutes

Ingredients:

- ⅓ cup Tapioca flour
- 2½ tablespoons Chile powder
- ¾ teaspoon Table salt (optional)
- 1¼ pounds Boneless country-style pork ribs, cut into 1½-inch chunks
- Vegetable oil spray

Directions:

1. Preheat the toaster oven to 375°F .

2. Mix the tapioca flour, chile powder, and salt (if using) in a large bowl until well combined. Add the country-style rib chunks and toss well to coat thoroughly.

3. When the machine is at temperature, gently shake off any excess tapioca coating from the chunks. Generously coat them on all sides with vegetable oil spray. Arrange the chunks in the air fryer oven in one (admittedly fairly tight) layer. The pieces may touch. Air-fry for 30 minutes, rearranging the pieces at the 10- and 20-minute marks to expose any touching bits, until very crisp and well browned.

4. Gently pour the contents of the pan onto a wire rack. Cool for 5 minutes before serving.

Chinese Pork And Vegetable Non-stir-fry

Servings: 4

Cooking Time: 30 Minutes

Ingredients:

- ➢ Seasoning sauce:
- ➢ 1 tablespoon soy sauce
- ➢ ¼ cup dry white wine
- ➢ 1 tablespoon sesame oil
- ➢ 1 tablespoon vegetable oil
- ➢ 1 teaspoon Chinese five-spice powder
- ➢ 2 6-ounce lean boneless pork chops cut into ¼ × 2-inch strips
- ➢ 1 1-pound package frozen vegetable mix or 2 cups sliced assorted fresh vegetables: broccoli, carrots, cauliflower, bell pepper, and the like
- ➢ 1 4-ounce can mushroom pieces, drained, or ½ cup cleaned and sliced fresh mushrooms
- ➢ 2 tablespoons sesame seeds
- ➢ 2 tablespoons minced fresh garlic

Directions:

1. Whisk together the seasoning sauce ingredients in a small bowl. Set aside.

2. Combine the pork, vegetables, mushrooms, sesame seeds, and garlic in an oiled or nonstick 8½ × 8½ × 2-inch square baking (cake) pan. Add the seasoning sauce ingredients and toss to coat the pork, vegetables, and mushrooms well.

3. BROIL for 30 minutes, turning with tongs every 8 minutes, until the vegetables and meat are well cooked and lightly browned.

Zesty London Broil

Servings: 4

Cooking Time: 28 Minutes

Ingredients:

- ⅔ cup ketchup
- ¼ cup honey
- ¼ cup olive oil
- 2 tablespoons apple cider vinegar
- 2 tablespoons Worcestershire sauce
- 2 tablespoons minced onion
- ½ teaspoon paprika
- 1 teaspoon salt
- 1 teaspoon freshly ground black pepper
- 2 pounds London broil, top round or flank steak (about 1-inch thick)

Directions:

1. Combine the ketchup, honey, olive oil, apple cider vinegar, Worcestershire sauce, minced onion, paprika, salt and pepper in a small bowl and whisk together.

2. Generously pierce both sides of the meat with a fork or meat tenderizer and place it in a shallow dish. Pour the marinade mixture over the steak, making sure all sides of the meat get coated with the marinade. Cover and refrigerate overnight.

3. Preheat the toaster oven to 400°F.

4. Transfer the London broil to the air fryer oven and air-fry for 28 minutes, depending on how rare or well done you like your steak. Flip the steak over halfway through the cooking time.

5. Remove the London broil from the air fryer oven and let it rest for five minutes on a cutting board. To serve, thinly slice the meat against the grain and transfer to a serving platter.

Bourbon Broiled Steak

Servings: 2

Cooking Time: 14 Minutes

Ingredients:

- ➤ Brushing mixture:
- ➤ ¼ cup bourbon
- ➤ 1 teaspoon garlic powder
- ➤ 1 tablespoon olive oil
- ➤ 1 teaspoon soy sauce
- ➤ 2 6- to 8-ounce sirloin steaks, ¾ inch thick

Directions:

1. Combine the brushing mixture ingredients in a small bowl. Brush the steaks on both sides with the mixture and place on the broiling rack with a pan underneath.

2. BROIL 4 minutes, remove from the oven, turn with tongs, brush the top and sides, and broil again for 4 minutes, or until done to your preference. To use the brushing mixture as a sauce or gravy, pour the mixture into a baking pan.

3. BROIL the mixture for 6 minutes, or until it begins to bubble.

Smokehouse-style Beef Ribs

Servings: 3

Cooking Time: 25 Minutes

Ingredients:

- ¼ teaspoon Mild smoked paprika
- ¼ teaspoon Garlic powder
- ¼ teaspoon Onion powder
- ¼ teaspoon Table salt
- ¼ teaspoon Ground black pepper
- 3 10- to 12-ounce beef back ribs (not beef short ribs)

Directions:

1. Preheat the toaster oven to 350°F .

2. Mix the smoked paprika, garlic powder, onion powder, salt, and pepper in a small bowl until uniform. Massage and pat this mixture onto the ribs.

3. When the machine is at temperature, set the ribs in the air fryer oven in one layer, turning them on their sides if necessary, sort of like they're spooning but with at least ¼ inch air space between them. Air-fry for 25 minutes, turning once, until deep brown and sizzling.

4. Use kitchen tongs to transfer the ribs to a wire rack. Cool for 5 minutes before serving.

Lime And Cumin Lamb Kebabs

Servings: 4

Cooking Time: 16 Minutes

Ingredients:

- ➢ 1 pound boneless lean lamb, trimmed and cut into 1 × 1-inch pieces
- ➢ 2 plum tomatoes, cut into 2 × 2-inch pieces
- ➢ 1 bell pepper, cut into 2 × 2-inch pieces
- ➢ 1 small onion, cut into 2 × 2-inch pieces
- ➢ Brushing mixture:
- ➢ ¼ cup lime juice
- ➢ ½ teaspoon soy sauce
- ➢ 1 tablespoon honey
- ➢ 1½ teaspoon ground cumin

Directions:

1. Skewer alternating pieces of lamb, tomato, pepper, and onion on four 9-inch skewers.

2. Combine the brushing mixture ingredients in a small bowl and brush on the kebabs. Place the skewers on a broiling rack with a pan underneath.

3. BROIL for 8 minutes. Turn the skewers, brush the kebabs with the mixture, and broil for 8 minutes, or until the meat and vegetables are cooked and browned.

Pesto Pork Chops

Servings: 2

Cooking Time: 15 Minutes

Ingredients:

- 2 (6-ounce) boneless pork loin chops
- 2 tablespoons basil pesto

Directions:

1. Preheat the toaster oven to 375°F on AIR FRY for 5 minutes.
2. Rub the pork chops all over with the pesto and set aside for 15 minutes.
3. Place the air-fryer basket in the baking tray and arrange the pork in the basket with no overlap.
4. In position 2, air fry for 15 minutes, turning halfway through, until the chops are lightly browned and have an internal temperature of 145°F.
5. Let the meat rest for 10 minutes and serve.

Crispy Smoked Pork Chops

Servings: 3

Cooking Time: 8 Minutes

Ingredients:

- ⅔ cup All-purpose flour or tapioca flour
- 1 Large egg white(s)
- 2 tablespoons Water
- 1½ cups Corn flake crumbs (gluten-free, if a concern)
- 3 ½-pound, ½-inch-thick bone-in smoked pork chops

Directions:

1. Preheat the toaster oven to 375°F.

2. Set up and fill three shallow soup plates or small pie plates on your counter: one for the flour; one for the egg white(s), whisked with the water until foamy; and one for the corn flake crumbs.

3. Set a chop in the flour and turn it several times, coating both sides and the edges. Gently shake off any excess flour, then set it in the beaten egg white mixture. Turn to coat both sides as well as the edges. Let any excess egg white slip back into the rest, then set the chop in the corn flake crumbs. Turn it several times, pressing gently to coat the chop evenly on both sides and around the edge. Set the chop aside and continue coating the remaining chop(s) in the same way.

4. Set the chops in the air fryer oven with as much air space between them as possible. Air-fry undisturbed for 8 minutes, or until the coating is crunchy and the chops are heated through.

5. Use kitchen tongs to transfer the chops to a wire rack and cool for a couple of minutes before serving.

Steak With Herbed Butter

Servings: 2

Cooking Time: 16 Minutes

Ingredients:

- 4 tablespoons unsalted butter, softened
- 1 tablespoon minced flat-leaf (Italian) parsley
- 1 tablespoon chopped fresh chives
- 2 cloves garlic, minced
- 1 teaspoon Worcestershire sauce
- 2 beef strip steaks, cut about 1 ½ inches thick
- 1 tablespoon olive oil
- Kosher salt and freshly ground black pepper

Directions:

1. Combine the butter, parsley, chives, garlic, and Worcestershire sauce in a small bowl until well blended; set aside.

2. Preheat the toaster oven to broil.

3. Brush the steaks with olive oil and season with salt and pepper. Place the steak on the broiler rack set over the broiler pan. Place the pan in the toaster oven, positioning the steaks about 3 to 4 inches below the heating element. (Depending on your oven and the thickness of the steak, you may need to set the rack to the middle position.) Broil for 6 minutes, turn the steaks over, and broil for an additional 7 minutes. If necessary to reach the desired doneness, turn the steaks over again and broil for an additional 3 minutes or until you reach your desired doneness.

4. Spread the herb butter generously over the steaks. Allow the steaks to stand for 5 to 10 minutes before slicing and serving.

Wasabi-coated Pork Loin Chops

Servings: 3

Cooking Time: 14 Minutes

Ingredients:

- 1½ cups Wasabi peas
- ¼ cup Plain panko bread crumbs
- 1 Large egg white(s)
- 2 tablespoons Water
- 3 5- to 6-ounce boneless center-cut pork loin chops (about ½ inch thick)

Directions:

1. Preheat the toaster oven to 375°F .

2. Put the wasabi peas in a food processor. Cover and process until finely ground, about like panko bread crumbs. Add the bread crumbs and pulse a few times to blend.

3. Set up and fill two shallow soup plates or small pie plates on your counter: one for the egg white(s), whisked with the water until uniform; and one for the wasabi pea mixture.

4. Dip a pork chop in the egg white mixture, coating the chop on both sides as well as around the edge. Allow any excess egg white mixture to slip back into the rest, then set the chop in the wasabi pea mixture. Press gently and turn it several times to coat evenly on both sides and around the edge. Set aside, then dip and coat the remaining chop(s).

5. Set the chops in the air fryer oven with as much air space between them as possible. Air-fry, turning once at the 6-minute mark, for 12 minutes, or until the chops are crisp and browned and an instant-read meat thermometer inserted into the center of a chop registers 145°F. If the machine is at 360°F, you may need to add 2 minutes to the cooking time.

6. Use kitchen tongs to transfer the chops to a wire rack. Cool for a couple of minutes before serving.

Italian Meatballs

Servings: 4

Cooking Time: 12 Minutes

Ingredients:

- 12 ounces lean ground beef
- 4 ounces Italian sausage, casing removed
- ½ cup breadcrumbs
- 1 cup grated Parmesan cheese
- 1 egg
- 2 tablespoons milk
- 2 teaspoons Italian seasoning
- ½ teaspoon onion powder
- ½ teaspoon garlic powder
- Pinch of red pepper flakes

Directions:

1. In a large bowl, place all the ingredients and mix well. Roll out 24 meatballs.

2. Preheat the toaster oven to 360°F.

3. Place the meatballs in the air fryer oven and air-fry for 12 minutes, tossing every 4 minutes. Using a food thermometer, check to ensure the internal temperature of the meatballs is 165°F.

Lamb Burger With Feta And Olives

Servings: 3   Cooking Time: 16 Minutes

Ingredients:

- 2 teaspoons olive oil
- ⅓ onion, finely chopped
- 1 clove garlic, minced
- 1 pound ground lamb
- 2 tablespoons fresh parsley, finely chopped
- 1½ teaspoons fresh oregano, finely chopped
- ½ cup black olives, finely chopped
- ⅓ cup crumbled feta cheese
- ½ teaspoon salt
- freshly ground black pepper
- 4 thick pita breads
- toppings and condiments

Directions:

1. Preheat a medium skillet over medium-high heat on the stovetop. Add the olive oil and cook the onion until tender, but not browned – about 4 to 5 minutes. Add the garlic and air-fry for another minute. Transfer the onion and garlic to a mixing bowl and add the ground lamb, parsley, oregano, olives, feta cheese, salt and pepper. Gently mix the ingredients together.

2. Divide the mixture into 3 or 4 equal portions and then form the hamburgers, being careful not to over-handle the meat. One good way to do this is to throw the meat back and forth between your hands like a baseball, packing the meat each time you catch it. Flatten the balls into patties, making an indentation in the center of each patty. Flatten the sides of the patties as well to make it easier to fit them into the air fryer oven.

3. Preheat the toaster oven to 370°F.

4. If you don't have room for all four burgers, air-fry two or three burgers at a time for 8 minutes at 370°F. Flip the burgers over and air-fry for another 8 minutes. If you cooked your burgers in batches, return the first batch of burgers to the air fryer oven for the last two minutes of cooking to re-heat. This should give you a medium-well burger. If you'd prefer a medium-rare burger, shorten the cooking time to about 13 minutes. Remove the burgers to a resting plate and let the burgers rest for a few minutes before dressing and serving.

5. While the burgers are resting, toast the pita breads in the air fryer oven for 2 minutes. Tuck the burgers into the toasted pita breads, or wrap the pitas around the burgers and serve with a tzatziki sauce or some mayonnaise.

Beef Vegetable Stew

Servings: 4

Cooking Time: 120 Minutes

Ingredients:

- 1 pound lean stewing beef, cut into 1-inch chunks
- 2 carrots, diced
- 2 celery stalks
- 1 large potato, diced
- ½ sweet onion, chopped
- 2 teaspoons minced garlic
- 1 (15-ounce) can diced tomatoes, with juices
- 1 teaspoon sea salt
- ½ teaspoon freshly ground black pepper
- 1 cup low-sodium beef broth
- 3 tablespoons all-purpose flour
- 1 cup frozen peas

Directions:

1. Place the rack in position 1 and preheat the toaster oven to 375°F on BAKE for 5 minutes.

2. In a 1½-quart casserole dish, combine the beef, carrots, celery, potato, onion, garlic, tomatoes, salt, and pepper.

3. In a small bowl, stir the broth and flour until well combined. Add the broth mixture to the beef mixture and stir to combine.

4. Cover with foil or a lid and bake for 2 hours, stirring each time you reset the timer, until the meat is very tender.

5. Stir in the peas and let stand for 10 minutes. Serve.

VEGETABLES AND VEGETARIAN

Rosemary Roasted Potatoes With Lemon

Servings: 12

Cooking Time: 4 Minutes

Ingredients:

- ➢ 1 pound small red-skinned potatoes, halved or cut into bite-sized chunks
- ➢ 1 tablespoon olive oil
- ➢ 1 teaspoon finely chopped fresh rosemary
- ➢ ¼ teaspoon salt
- ➢ freshly ground black pepper
- ➢ 1 tablespoon lemon zest

Directions:

1. Preheat the toaster oven to 400°F.

2. Toss the potatoes with the olive oil, rosemary, salt and freshly ground black pepper.

3. Air-fry for 12 minutes (depending on the size of the chunks), tossing the potatoes a few times throughout the cooking process.

4. As soon as the potatoes are tender to a knifepoint, toss them with the lemon zest and more salt if desired.

Baked Mac And Cheese

Servings: 4

Cooking Time: 45 Minutes

Ingredients:

- Oil spray (hand-pumped)
- 1½ cups whole milk, room temperature
- ½ cup heavy (whipping) cream, room temperature
- 1 cup shredded cheddar cheese
- 4 ounces cream cheese, room temperature
- ½ teaspoon dry mustard
- ⅛ teaspoon sea salt
- ⅛ teaspoon freshly ground black pepper
- 1¼ cups dried elbow macaroni
- ¼ cup bread crumbs
- 2 tablespoons grated Parmesan cheese
- 1 tablespoon salted butter, melted

Directions:

1. Place the rack in position 1 and preheat the toaster oven to 375°F on CONVECTION BAKE for 5 minutes.

2. Lightly coat an 8-inch-square baking dish with the oil spray.

3. In a large bowl, stir the milk, cream, cheddar, cream cheese, mustard, salt, and pepper until well combined.

4. Transfer the mixture to the baking dish, stir in the macaroni and cover tightly with foil.

5. Bake for 35 minutes.

6. While the macaroni is baking, in a small bowl, stir the bread crumbs, Parmesan, and butter to form coarse crumbs. Set aside.

7. Take the baking dish out of the oven, uncover, stir, and evenly cover with the bread crumb mixture.

8. Bake uncovered for an additional 10 minutes until the pasta is tender, bubbly, and golden brown. Serve.

Blistered Green Beans

Servings: 3

Cooking Time: 10 Minutes

Ingredients:

➢ ¾ pound Green beans, trimmed on both ends

➢ 1½ tablespoons Olive oil

➢ 3 tablespoons Pine nuts

➢ 1½ tablespoons Balsamic vinegar

➢ 1½ teaspoons Minced garlic

➢ ¾ teaspoon Table salt

➢ ¾ teaspoon Ground black pepper

Directions:

1. Preheat the toaster oven to 400°F.

2. Toss the green beans and oil in a large bowl until all the green beans are glistening.

3. When the machine is at temperature, pile the green beans into the air fryer oven. Air-fry for 10 minutes, tossing often to rearrange the green beans in the air fryer oven, or until blistered and tender.

4. Dump the contents of the air fryer oven into a serving bowl. Add the pine nuts, vinegar, garlic, salt, and pepper. Toss well to coat and combine. Serve warm or at room temperature.

Roasted Ratatouille Vegetables

Servings: 15

Cooking Time: 2 Minutes

Ingredients:

- 1 baby or Japanese eggplant, cut into 1½-inch cubes
- 1 red pepper, cut into 1-inch chunks
- 1 yellow pepper, cut into 1-inch chunks
- 1 zucchini, cut into 1-inch chunks
- 1 clove garlic, minced
- ½ teaspoon dried basil
- 1 tablespoon olive oil
- salt and freshly ground black pepper
- ¼ cup sliced sun-dried tomatoes in oil
- 2 tablespoons chopped fresh basil

Directions:

1. Preheat the toaster oven to 400°F.

2. Toss the eggplant, peppers and zucchini with the garlic, dried basil, olive oil, salt and freshly ground black pepper.

3. Air-fry the vegetables at 400°F for 15 minutes.

4. As soon as the vegetables are tender, toss them with the sliced sun-dried tomatoes and fresh basil and serve.

Tasty Golden Potatoes

Servings: 4

Cooking Time: 38 Minutes

Ingredients:

- 2 cups peeled and shredded potatoes
- ½ cup peeled and shredded carrots
- ¼ cup shredded onion
- 1 teaspoon salt
- 1 teaspoon dried rosemary
- 1 teaspoon dried cumin
- 3 tablespoons vegetable oil
- Salt and freshly ground black pepper to taste

Directions:

1. Preheat the toaster oven to 400° F.
2. Mix all the ingredients together in a 1-quart 8½ × 8½ × 2-inch ovenproof baking dish. Adjust the seasonings to taste. Cover the dish with aluminum foil.
3. BAKE, covered, for 30 minutes, or until tender. Remove the cover.
4. BROIL for 8 minutes, or until the top is browned.

Yellow Squash With Bell Peppers

Servings: 4

Cooking Time: 50 Minutes

Ingredients:

➢ Squash mixture:

➢ 2 cups yellow (summer) squash, thinly sliced

➢ ⅓ cup dry white wine

➢ 1 bell pepper, seeded and sliced into thin strips

➢ 1 6½-ounce jar marinated artichoke hearts, drained and sliced

➢ 1 tablespoon minced fresh garlic

➢ 1 5-ounce can diced pimientos, drained

➢ Salt and freshly ground black pepper to taste

➢ ¼ cup shredded part-skim mozzarella cheese

➢ 3 tablespoons Homemade Bread Crumbs

➢ 2 tablespoons chopped fresh cilantro

Directions:

1. Preheat the toaster oven to 400° F.

2. Combine the squash mixture ingredients in a 1-quart 8½ × 8½ × 4-inch ovenproof baking dish, mixing well. Adjust the seasonings.

3. BAKE, covered, for 40 minutes, or until the vegetables are tender. Uncover and sprinkle with the cheese and bread crumbs.

4. BROIL 10 minutes, or until the top is lightly browned. Garnish with the chopped cilantro before serving.

Street Corn

Servings: 4

Cooking Time: 10 Minutes

Ingredients:

- ➢ 1 tablespoon butter
- ➢ 4 ears corn
- ➢ ⅓ cup plain Greek yogurt
- ➢ 2 tablespoons Parmesan cheese
- ➢ ½ teaspoon paprika
- ➢ ½ teaspoon garlic powder
- ➢ ¼ teaspoon salt
- ➢ ¼ teaspoon black pepper
- ➢ ¼ cup finely chopped cilantro

Directions:

1. Preheat the toaster oven to 400°F.

2. In a medium microwave-safe bowl, melt the butter in the microwave. Lightly brush the outside of the ears of corn with the melted butter.

3. Place the corn into the air fryer oven and air-fry for 5 minutes, flip the corn, and cook another 5 minutes.

4. Meanwhile, in a medium bowl, mix the yogurt, cheese, paprika, garlic powder, salt, and pepper. Set aside.

5. Carefully remove the corn from the air fryer oven and let cool 3 minutes. Brush the outside edges with the yogurt mixture and top with fresh chopped cilantro. Serve immediately.

Crispy Herbed Potatoes

Servings: 6

Cooking Time: 20 Minutes

Ingredients:

- ➢ 3 medium baking potatoes, washed and cubed
- ➢ ½ teaspoon dried thyme
- ➢ 1 teaspoon minced dried rosemary
- ➢ ½ teaspoon garlic powder
- ➢ 1 teaspoon sea salt
- ➢ ½ teaspoon black pepper
- ➢ 2 tablespoons extra-virgin olive oil
- ➢ ¼ cup chopped parsley

Directions:

1. Preheat the toaster oven to 390°F.
2. Pat the potatoes dry. In a large bowl, mix together the cubed potatoes, thyme, rosemary, garlic powder, sea salt, and pepper. Drizzle and toss with olive oil.
3. Pour the herbed potatoes into the air fryer oven. Air-fry for 20 minutes, stirring every 5 minutes.
4. Toss the cooked potatoes with chopped parsley and serve immediately.
5. VARY IT! Potatoes are versatile — add any spice or seasoning mixture you prefer and create your own favorite side dish.

Roasted Veggie Kebabs

Servings: 4

Cooking Time: 45 Minutes

Ingredients:

➢ Brushing mixture:

➢ 3 tablespoons olive oil

➢ 1 tablespoon soy sauce

➢ 1 teaspoon garlic powder

➢ 1 teaspoon ground cumin

➢ 2 tablespoons balsamic vinegar

➢ Salt and freshly ground black pepper to taste

➢ Cauliflower, zucchini, onion, broccoli, bell pepper, mushrooms, celery, cabbage, beets, and the like, cut into approximately 2 × 2-inch pieces

Directions:

1. Preheat the toaster oven to 400° F.

2. Combine the brushing mixture ingredients in a small bowl, mixing well. Set aside.

3. Skewer the vegetable pieces on 4 9-inch metal skewers and place the skewers lengthwise on a broiling rack with a pan underneath.

4. BAKE for 40 minutes, or until the vegetables are tender, brushing with the mixture every 10 minutes.

5. BROIL for 5 minutes, or until lightly browned.

Tandoori Cauliflower

Servings: 4

Cooking Time: 10 Minutes

Ingredients:

- ½ cup Plain full-fat yogurt (not Greek yogurt)
- 1½ teaspoons Yellow curry powder, purchased or homemade
- 1½ teaspoons Lemon juice
- ¾ teaspoon Table salt (optional)
- 4½ cups (about 1 pound 2 ounces) 2-inch cauliflower florets

Directions:

1. Preheat the toaster oven to 400°F.

2. Whisk the yogurt, curry powder, lemon juice, and salt (if using) in a large bowl until uniform. Add the florets and stir gently to coat the florets well and evenly. Even better, use your clean, dry hands to get the yogurt mixture down into all the nooks of the florets.

3. When the machine is at temperature, transfer the florets to the air fryer oven, spreading them gently into as close to one layer as you can. Air-fry for 10 minutes, tossing and rearranging the florets twice so that any covered or touching parts are exposed to the air currents, until lightly browned and tender if still a bit crunchy.

4. Pour the contents of the air fryer oven onto a wire rack. Cool for at least 5 minutes before serving, or serve at room temperature.

Asparagus Ronald

Servings: 4

Cooking Time: 25 Minutes

Ingredients:

- ➢ 20 asparagus spears, rinsed and hard stem ends cut off
- ➢ 1 tablespoon soy sauce
- ➢ 3 tablespoons lemon juice
- ➢ 3 tablespoons olive oil
- ➢ Salt and freshly ground black pepper
- ➢ 3 tablespoons crumbled feta cheese

Directions:

1. Preheat the toaster oven to 400° F.

2. Place the asparagus spears in a 1-quart 8½ × 8½ × 4-inch ovenproof baking dish.

3. Drizzle the soy sauce, lemon juice, and olive oil over the asparagus spears. Season to taste with salt and pepper. Cover the dish with aluminum foil.

4. BAKE for 25 minutes, or until tender. Sprinkle with the feta cheese before serving.

Grits Casserole

Servings: 4

Cooking Time: 30 Minutes

Ingredients:

- 10 fresh asparagus spears, cut into 1-inch pieces
- 2 cups cooked grits, cooled to room temperature
- 1 egg, beaten
- 2 teaspoons Worcestershire sauce
- ½ teaspoon garlic powder
- ¼ teaspoon salt
- 2 slices provolone cheese (about 1½ ounces)
- oil for misting or cooking spray

Directions:

1. Mist asparagus spears with oil and air-fry at 390°F for 5 minutes, until crisp-tender.
2. In a medium bowl, mix together the grits, egg, Worcestershire, garlic powder, and salt.
3. Spoon half of grits mixture into air fryer oven baking pan and top with asparagus.
4. Tear cheese slices into pieces and layer evenly on top of asparagus.
5. Top with remaining grits.
6. Bake at 360°F for 25 minutes. The casserole will rise a little as it cooks. When done, the top will have browned lightly with just a hint of crispiness.

Crispy, Cheesy Leeks

Servings: 4

Cooking Time: 15 Minutes

Ingredients:

➢ 2 Medium leek(s), about 9 ounces each

➢ Olive oil spray

➢ ¼ cup Seasoned Italian-style dried bread crumbs (gluten-free, if a concern)

➢ ¼ cup (about ¾ ounce) Finely grated Parmesan cheese

➢ 2 tablespoons Olive oil

Directions:

1. Preheat the toaster oven to 350°F .

2. Trim off the root end of the leek(s) as well as the dark green top(s), leaving about a 5-inch usable section. Split the leek section(s) in half lengthwise. Set the leek halves cut side up on your work surface. Pull out and remove in one piece the semicircles that make up the inner structure of the leek, about halfway down. Set the removed "inside" next to the outer leek "shells" on your cutting board. Generously coat them all on all sides (particularly the "bottoms") with olive oil spray.

3. Set the leeks and their insides cut side up in the air fryer oven with as much air space between them as possible. Air-fry undisturbed for 12 minutes.

4. Meanwhile, mix the bread crumbs, cheese, and olive oil in a small bowl until well combined.

5. After 12 minutes in the air fryer oven, sprinkle this mixture inside the leek shells and on top of the leek insides. Increase the machine's temperature to 375°F (or 380°F or 390°F, if one of these is the closest setting). Air-fry undisturbed for 3 minutes, or until the topping is lightly browned.

6. Use a nonstick-safe spatula to transfer the leeks to a serving platter. Cool for a few minutes before serving warm.

DESSERTS

Dark Chocolate Peanut Butter S'mores

Servings: 4

Cooking Time: 6 Minutes

Ingredients:

- ➢ 4 graham cracker sheets
- ➢ 4 marshmallows
- ➢ 4 teaspoons chunky peanut butter
- ➢ 4 ounces dark chocolate
- ➢ ½ teaspoon ground cinnamon

Directions:

1. Preheat the toaster oven to 390°F. Break the graham crackers in half so you have 8 pieces.

2. Place 4 pieces of graham cracker on the bottom of the air fryer oven. Top each with one of the marshmallows and bake for 6 or 7 minutes, or until the marshmallows have a golden brown center.

3. While cooking, slather each of the remaining graham crackers with 1 teaspoon peanut butter.

4. When baking completes, carefully remove each of the graham crackers, add 1 ounce of dark chocolate on top of the marshmallow, and lightly sprinkle with cinnamon. Top with the remaining peanut butter graham cracker to make the sandwich. Serve immediately.

Make-ahead Chocolate Chip Cookies

Servings: 12

Cooking Time: 45 Minutes

Ingredients:

- 2⅛ cups (10⅔ ounces) all-purpose flour
- ½ teaspoon baking soda
- ½ teaspoon table salt
- 1 cup packed (7 ounces) light brown sugar
- ½ cup (3½ ounces)granulated sugar
- 12 tablespoons unsalted butter, melted and cooled
- 1 large egg plus 1 large yolk
- 2 teaspoons vanilla extract
- 1 cup (6 ounces) semisweet chocolate chips

Directions:

1. Adjust toaster oven rack to middle position and preheat the toaster oven to 350 degrees. Line large and small rimmed baking sheets with parchment paper. Whisk flour, baking soda, and salt together in bowl.

2. Whisk brown sugar and granulated sugar together in medium bowl. Whisk in melted butter until combined. Whisk in egg and yolk and vanilla until smooth. Gently stir in flour mixture with rubber spatula until soft dough forms. Fold in chocolate chips.

3. Working with 2 tablespoons dough at a time, roll into balls. Space desired number of dough balls at least 1½ inches apart on prepared small sheet; space remaining dough balls evenly on prepared large sheet. Using bottom of greased dry measuring cup, press each ball until 2 inches in diameter.

4. Bake small sheet of cookies until edges are just beginning to brown and centers are soft and puffy, 10 to 15 minutes. Let cookies cool slightly on sheet. Serve warm or at room temperature.

5. Freeze remaining large sheet of cookies until firm, about 1 hour. Transfer cookies to 1-gallon zipper-lock bag and freeze for up to 1 month. Bake frozen cookies as directed; do not thaw.

Little Swedish Coffee Cakes

Servings: 4

Cooking Time: 30 Minutes

Ingredients:

- Cake batter:
- 1 cup unbleached flour
- 1 teaspoon baking powder
- ½ cup sugar
- ½ cup finely ground pecans
- ¾ cup low-fat buttermilk
- 1 tablespoon vegetable oil
- 1 egg, lightly beaten
- 1 teaspoon vanilla extract
- Salt to taste
- Sifted confectioners' sugar
- Canola oil for brushing pan

Directions:

1. Preheat the toaster oven to 350° F.

2. Combine the cake batter ingredients in a bowl, mixing well. Pour the batter into an oiled or nonstick 8½ × 8½ × 2-inch square baking (cake) pan.

3. BAKE for 30 minutes, or until a toothpick inserted in the center comes out clean. Run a knife around the edge of the pan, invert, and place on a rack to cool. Sprinkle the top with sifted confectioners' sugar and cut into small squares.

Not Key Lime, Lime Pie

Servings: 3   Cooking Time: 27 Minutes

Ingredients:

- 1 tablespoon grated lime zest
- 3 large egg yolks
- 1 (14-ounce) can sweetened condensed milk
- ½ cup fresh lime juice
- 1 ¾ cups graham cracker crumbs (about 12 full graham crackers)
- ⅓ cup granulated sugar
- ⅛ teaspoon table salt
- ½ cup unsalted butter, melted
- Nonstick cooking spray
- WHIPPED CREAM
- 1 cup heavy cream
- ⅓ cup confectioners' sugar

Directions:

1. Preheat the toaster oven to 350°F.

2. Whisk the lime zest and egg yolks in a large bowl for 1 minute. Whisk in the sweetened condensed milk and lime juice. Set aside to thicken while you prepare the crust.

3. Stir the graham cracker crumbs, granulated sugar, and salt in a medium bowl. Pour the butter over the mixture and mix until combined and moist. Press the crust evenly into the bottom and up the sides of a 9-inch pie plate. Pack tightly using the back of a large spoon. Bake for 10 minutes. Let cool on a cooling rack.

4. When the crust is completely cool, pour the lime filling inside. Bake for 15 to 17 minutes, or until the center is set (it will still jiggle a bit). Allow the pie to cool completely at room temperature. Spray plastic wrap with nonstick cooking spray and place on the pie. Refrigerate for at least 3 hours or overnight.

5. Beat the cream in a large bowl with an electric mixer at medium-high speed until soft peaks form. Add the confectioners' sugar, one tablespoon at a time, and continue to beat until stiff peaks form. Dollop, pipe, or spread the whipped cream over the pie before serving. Refrigerate leftovers for up to 3 days.

Orange Strawberry Flan

Servings: 4

Cooking Time: 45 Minutes

Ingredients:

- ¼ cup sugar
- ½ cup concentrated orange juice
- 1 12-ounce can low-fat evaporated milk
- 3 egg yolks
- 1 cup frozen strawberries, thawed and sliced, or 1 cup fresh strawberries, washed, stemmed, and sliced
- 4 fresh mint sprigs

Directions:

1. Preheat the toaster oven to 375° F.

2. Place the sugar in a baking pan and broil for 4 minutes, or until the sugar melts. Remove from the oven, stir briefly, and pour equal portions of the caramelized sugar into four 1-cup-size ovenproof dishes. Set aside.

3. Blend the orange juice, evaporated milk, and egg yolks in a food processor or blender until smooth. Transfer the mixture to a medium bowl and fold in the sliced strawberries. Pour the mixture in equal portions into the four dishes.

4. BAKE for 45 minutes, or until a knife inserted in the center comes out clean. Chill for several hours. The flan may be loosened by running a knife around the edge and inverted on individual plates or served in the dishes. Garnish with fresh mint sprigs.

Fried Snickers Bars

Servings: 8

Cooking Time: 4 Minutes

Ingredients:

- ⅓ cup All-purpose flour
- 1 Large egg white(s), beaten until foamy
- 1½ cups (6 ounces) Vanilla wafer cookie crumbs
- 8 Fun-size (0.6-ounce/17-gram) Snickers bars, frozen
- Vegetable oil spray

Directions:

1. Preheat the toaster oven to 400°F.

2. Set up and fill three shallow soup plates or small pie plates on your counter: one for the flour, one for the beaten egg white(s), and one for the cookie crumbs.

3. Unwrap the frozen candy bars. Dip one in the flour, turning it to coat on all sides. Gently stir any excess, then set it in the beaten egg white(s). Turn it to coat all sides, even the ends, then let any excess egg white slip back into the rest. Set the candy bar in the cookie crumbs. Turn to coat on all sides, even the ends. Dip the candy bar back in the egg white(s) a second time, then into the cookie crumbs a second time, making sure you have an even coating all around. Coat the covered candy bar all over with vegetable oil spray. Set aside so you can dip and coat the remaining candy bars.

4. Set the coated candy bars in the pan with as much air space between them as possible. Air-fry undisturbed for 4 minutes, or until golden brown.

5. Remove the pan from the machine and let the candy bars cool in the pan for 10 minutes. Use a nonstick-safe spatula to transfer them to a wire rack and cool for 5 minutes more before chowing down.

Chewy Brownies

Servings: 16

Cooking Time: 60 Minutes

Ingredients:

- ➢ 3 tablespoons Dutch-processed cocoa powder
- ➢ ¾ teaspoon espresso powder (optional)
- ➢ ⅓ cup boiling water
- ➢ 1 ounce unsweetened chocolate, chopped fine
- ➢ 5 tablespoons vegetable oil
- ➢ 2 tablespoons unsalted butter, melted and cooled
- ➢ 1¼ cups (8¾ ounces) sugar
- ➢ 1 large egg plus 1 large yolk
- ➢ 1 teaspoon vanilla extract
- ➢ ¾ cup (3¾ ounces) plus 2 tablespoons all-purpose flour
- ➢ 3 ounces bittersweet chocolate, cut into ½-inch pieces
- ➢ ½ teaspoon table salt

Directions:

1. Adjust toaster oven rack to middle position and preheat the toaster oven to 350 degrees. Make foil sling for 8-inch square baking pan by folding 2 long sheets of aluminum foil so each is 8 inches wide. Lay sheets of foil in pan perpendicular to each other, with extra foil hanging over edges of pan. Push foil into corners and up sides of pan, smoothing foil flush to pan. Spray foil with vegetable oil spray.

2. Whisk cocoa; espresso powder, if using; and boiling water together in large bowl until smooth. Add unsweetened chocolate and whisk until chocolate is melted. Whisk in oil and melted butter. (Mixture may look curdled.) Whisk in sugar, egg and yolk, and vanilla until smooth. Add flour, bittersweet chocolate, and salt and mix with rubber spatula until no dry flour remains.

3. Scrape batter into prepared pan, smooth top, and bake until toothpick inserted in center comes out with few moist crumbs attached, 25 to 30 minutes, rotating dish halfway through baking. Transfer pan to wire rack and cool for 1½ hours.

4. Using foil overhang, lift brownies from pan. Return brownies to wire rack and let cool completely, about 1 hour. Cut into 2-inch squares and serve.

Hasselback Apple Crisp

Servings: 4

Cooking Time: 20 Minutes

Ingredients:

- 2 large Gala apples, peeled, cored and cut in half
- ¼ cup butter, melted
- ½ teaspoon ground cinnamon
- 2 tablespoons sugar
- Topping
- 3 tablespoons butter, melted
- 2 tablespoons brown sugar
- ¼ cup chopped pecans
- 2 tablespoons rolled oats
- 1 tablespoon flour
- vanilla ice cream
- caramel sauce

Directions:

1. Place the apples cut side down on a cutting board. Slicing from stem end to blossom end, make 8 to 10 slits down the apple halves but only slice three quarters of the way through the apple, not all the way through to the cutting board.

2. Preheat the toaster oven to 330°F and pour a little water into the bottom of the air fryer oven drawer. (This will help prevent the grease that drips into the bottom drawer from burning and smoking.)

3. Transfer the apples to the air fryer oven, flat side down. Combine ¼ cup of melted butter, cinnamon and sugar in a small bowl. Brush this butter mixture onto the apples and air-fry at 330°F for 15 minutes. Baste the apples several times with the butter mixture during the cooking process.

4. While the apples are air-frying, make the filling. Combine 3 tablespoons of melted butter with the brown sugar, pecans, rolled oats and flour in a bowl. Stir with a fork until the mixture resembles small crumbles.

5. When the timer on the air fryer oven is up, spoon the topping down the center of the apples. Air-fry at 330°F for an additional 5 minutes.

6. Transfer the apples to a serving plate and serve with vanilla ice cream and caramel sauce.

Carrot Cake

Servings: 6 — Cooking Time: 30 Minutes

Ingredients:

- ➢ FOR THE CAKE
- ➢ ½ cup canola oil, plus extra for greasing the baking dish
- ➢ 1 cup all-purpose flour, plus extra for dusting the baking dish
- ➢ 1 cup granulated sugar
- ➢ 1 teaspoon baking powder
- ➢ ½ teaspoon sea salt
- ➢ 2 teaspoons pumpkin pie spice
- ➢ 2 large eggs
- ➢ 1 cup carrot, finely shredded
- ➢ ½ cup dried apricot, chopped
- ➢ FOR THE ICING
- ➢ 4 ounces cream cheese, room temperature
- ➢ ¼ cup salted butter, room temperature
- ➢ 1 teaspoon vanilla extract
- ➢ 2 cups confectioners' sugar

Directions:

1. To make the cake
2. Place the rack in position 1 and preheat the oven to 325°F on BAKE for 5 minutes.
3. Lightly grease an 8-inch-square baking dish with oil and dust with flour.
4. Place the rack in position 1.
5. In a large bowl, stir the flour, sugar, baking powder, salt, and pumpkin pie spice.
6. Make a well in the center and add the oil and eggs, stirring until just combined. Add the carrot and apricot and stir until well mixed.
7. Transfer the batter to the baking dish and bake for about 30 minutes until golden brown and a toothpick inserted in the center comes out clean.
8. Remove the cake from the oven and cool completely in the baking dish.
9. To make the icing
10. When the cake is cool, whisk the cream cheese, butter, and vanilla until very smooth and blended. Add the confectioners' sugar and whisk until creamy and thick, about 2 minutes.
11. Ice the cake and serve.

White Chocolate Cranberry Blondies

Servings: 6

Cooking Time: 18 Minutes

Ingredients:

- ⅓ cup butter
- ½ cup sugar
- 1 teaspoon vanilla extract
- 1 large egg
- 1 cup all-purpose flour
- ½ teaspoon baking powder
- ⅛ teaspoon salt
- ¼ cup dried cranberries
- ¼ cup white chocolate chips

Directions:

1. Preheat the toaster oven to 320°F.
2. In a large bowl, cream the butter with the sugar and vanilla extract. Whisk in the egg and set aside.
3. In a separate bowl, mix the flour with the baking powder and salt. Then gently mix the dry ingredients into the wet. Fold in the cranberries and chocolate chips.
4. Liberally spray an oven-safe 7-inch springform pan with olive oil and pour the batter into the pan.
5. Air-fry for 17 minutes or until a toothpick inserted in the center comes out clean.
6. Remove and let cool 5 minutes before serving.

Printed by Libri Plureos GmbH in Hamburg, Germany